Living Words

Stephanie Dowrick has been a life-long reader, as well as editor, publisher, teacher of creative writing, and writer. Her work encompasses bestselling fiction — *Running Backwards Over Sand* and *Tasting Salt* — as well as internationally renowned works of non-fiction, including *Intimacy and Solitude*, *Forgiveness and Other Acts of Love*, *The Universal Heart* and *Every Day a New Beginning*. She is also known for her teaching, workshops and broadcasts on psychological, spiritual and ethical issues, and especially for her contributions to ABC Radio National's 'Life Matters' and to *Good Weekend* magazine, where she has been a columnist since 2001. Stephanie was born in New Zealand, worked in London for many years, where she was founder of The Women's Press, and has made her home in Sydney since 1983. She has two young adult children.

To write to Stephanie Dowrick or learn more about her work, you may access her web site at www.stephaniedowrick.com

Also by Stephanie Dowrick

Non-Fiction
Land of Zeus
Intimacy and Solitude
The Intimacy and Solitude Self-Therapy Book
Forgiveness and Other Acts of Love
Daily Acts of Love
Daily Acts of Love: A Journal
The Universal Heart
Every Day a New Beginning

Fiction
Running Backwards Over Sand
Tasting Salt

Children's Fiction
Katherine Rose Says No

Audio
Intimacy and Solitude
Living with Change
The Humane Virtues
The Art of Acceptance
The Universal Heart
Guided Meditations: Grace & Courage (with Tony Backhouse)
Self-Love

Living Words

Journal writing for self-discovery, insight & creativity

Stephanie Dowrick

VIKING
an imprint of
Penguin Books

Viking

Published by the Penguin Group
Penguin Books Australia Ltd
250 Camberwell Road, Camberwell, Victoria 3124, Australia
Penguin Books Ltd
80 Strand, London WC2R 0RL, England
Penguin Putnam Inc.
375 Hudson Street, New York, New York 10014, USA
Penguin Books, a division of Pearson Canada
10 Alcorn Avenue, Toronto, Ontario, Canada M4V 3B2
Penguin Books (NZ) Ltd
Cnr Rosedale and Airborne Roads, Albany, Auckland, New Zealand
Penguin Books (South Africa) (Pty) Ltd
24 Sturdee Avenue, Rosebank, Johannesburg 2196, South Africa
Penguin Books India (P) Ltd
11, Community Centre, Panchsheel Park, New Delhi 110 017, India

First published by Penguin Books Australia Ltd 2003

10 9 8 7 6 5 4 3 2 1

Cover design by Penguin Design Studio
Text design by Danie Pout Design
Typeset in 12.5/16 pt Perpetua by Post Pre-press Group, Brisbane, Queensland
Printed and bound in Singapore by Imago Productions

National Library of Australia
Cataloguing-in-Publication data:

Dowrick, Stephanie.
    Living words: journal writing for self-discovery, insight and creativity.

    ISBN 0 670 04153 X.

    1. English language – Rhetoric – Handbooks, manuals, etc.
    2. Creative writing – Handbooks, manuals, etc. I. Title.

    808.042

www.penguin.com.au

Contents

LOVE THE QUESTIONS

'Try to love the questions themselves,
as if they were locked rooms or
books written in a very foreign language.'

Rainer Maria Rilke

Warming Up

Writing a journal may change your life

Are you ready for this?

I need to warn you: writing a journal can literally be life-changing. It can also be addictive, moving, illuminating and tremendous fun.

Journal writing is the key to discovering your own unique inner world. It can bring you a vast array of invaluable new insights. It lets you 'read' your own life. It lets you see the world around yourself more richly, more deeply. It can teach you to value your own history, values and opinions. (After all, no one knows you better than you know yourself. But sometimes you need ways to *discover* what you know.)

JOURNAL WRITING CAN GIVE YOU AN INVALUABLE SENSE OF BEING AT THE CENTRE OF YOUR LIFE RATHER THAN AT THE PERIPHERY. At the same time, it will make you less anxiously 'self-centred'. And it will let you know who and what are really important to you.

Journal writing can also make you grateful.

It can make you laugh, seethe, howl, rejoice.

It can make you honest.

It can give you a much greater sense of choice about how you are living your life. It can train you to observe all kinds of situations. And to learn something of value even from the unwelcome ones. (That may save you from going on repeating the same mistakes!)

Journal writing will hone your eye for beauty and let you re-experience wonder. It will let you intensify and renew your pleasure in events and situations that have gone well. It will give you an invaluable opportunity to deepen your creativity about all aspects of your life – not just writing. This will happen whether or not you write 'well' in the conventional sense. Writing 'well' is irrelevant here. Journal writing needs (and builds) insight, courage and humour. It needs tenacity. It needs truthfulness. That's all.

Journal writing gives you a significant break from comparing and competing – even with yourself. Certainly it deepens your capacity for discernment. But it also weans you away most gently from petty judgements and undermining self-criticism.

Journal writing frees your spirit. It liberates insight. And soothes your soul.

Writing a journal involves externalising your thoughts, ideas and impressions. It lets you see, in black and white, what your dreams and ideals are. It lets you record your deepest feelings and capture your experiences. You do this simply by writing them down freely and truthfully. You engage with them from the inside out. This process – and its outcome – are very different from keeping those same thoughts in your mind and turning them over and over by worrying or daydreaming. Putting them out there, onto the pages of your journal, shifts the energy of those thoughts in a distinct and most helpful way. It gives you an invaluable measure of distance between yourself and your thoughts. That makes it much easier to see what's really going on and how best to act – or not.

You can become curious about a complex situation rather than overwhelmed by it. You can find out what you really think and feel. You can find out what you want.

Capturing the patterns

Writing a journal also allows you to see the *patterns* of your own thinking, emotions and actions. (*Patterns* will include habits and routines: 'ways of seeing' that are automatic rather than fresh. It will also include assumptions and stale or static judgements. And habitual emotional reactions that may not be useful or even appropriate.)

Those patterns will emerge quite inevitably within a few months of journal writing. More than anything else, the unfolding of these patterns can empower you – not least to see where change is needed, where your behaviour is serving you well, or not.

The way that these patterns emerge surprises almost everyone. Lara explains this.

LARA

'I had no idea how little of my emotional energy and creativity went into my own life. It wasn't until I had been writing my journal for a few months that I really saw clearly how exclusively focused I was on other people's needs. That's a good thing, too, but I had left myself behind. I was looking at my own life through the prism of their needs only.

'Journal writing has been like switching on a light for me. I could see what I needed for myself – and I could see how bringing myself back into the picture and feeding my own creativity and "dream time" actually benefited my family and friends also. Even my attitude to work has changed. I'm more confident, but actually far more easygoing.'

Good reasons not to write a journal?

'Only teenage girls write journals.'

Teenage girls are often avid journal writers — and for good reasons. (I hope many will be using this journal.) The pity is that too many of us are persuaded to give up journal writing as we get older, often because we let ourselves be convinced that there are more important things to do, or that we should be attentive only to other people's lives and not to our own. So journal writing gets sacrificed, along with much of our sensitivity to the contours of our own unique existence.

If you begin journal writing in adolescence you usually do so quite instinctively, discovering how effectively it supports you to make sense of the outer world and your own often conflicting emotions and impressions. You may also use it as a brilliant way to 'get a handle on things'. You probably find it empowering to discover what you think and feel. And to learn how inevitably even the most powerful moods and emotions give way to something else. (Life itself moves through us always, changing things.)

It's true that in adolescence you may sometimes be highly focused on emotional events. It's also true that you may find it difficult to see things from other people's points of view. But journal writing helps with that. It gives you distance. It also lets you stop returning to the same unproductive thoughts over and over again. That's really helpful, however young or old you are.

The great thing about journal writing is that it is infinitely flexible. It comes to meet you at whatever stage of life or maturity you have reached. You have only to make yourself available to it.

'Adults have better things to do.'

It would be worth exploring in your journal whether or not you yet feel like an 'adult', or even know for sure what an adult is! Certainly most people I know who write a journal find that, without thinking about it very much and certainly without 'trying', they have learned to allocate their time with more skill and sensitivity than before they were journal writers.

We spend so much of our time absent from the present moment, responding to other people's cues without very much self-awareness. It's a bit like driving for hours, obeying all the traffic rules, but without noticing where you have actually been.

IT IS IMPOSSIBLE TO WRITE A JOURNAL AND NOT BECOME MORE SELF-AWARE, MORE IN TUNE WITH HOW YOU ARE SPENDING (OR WASTING) YOUR PRECIOUS LIFETIME. As the writing continues, this means that you become not only a more acute observer of your own life, but also a more acute observer of life itself.

What's more, this capacity to observe gives you inner balance, a greater sense of choice and certainly a most welcome freedom from the experience of being buffeted and tossed about by events and emotions. Here's how Candy sees it.

CANDY
'When I am in the process of actually writing about something, then I am usually totally absorbed in what I am doing. I am not thinking about it very consciously. I'm just getting it down. I am letting myself roll with it. But what I find fantastically useful is the space that exists between me and those emotions once I have got them down. I am noticing that it's a kind of relief to get things "out there" – onto the page. That's unexpectedly true even about quite pleasurable things. I sometimes feel like I am clearing my inner decks ready for the next new moment.

'I am definitely far more "present", moment by moment, since I have been journalling. I feel like I have greater curiosity, too, about my life. And I am certainly valuing it more. *Where is it going next? Where am I going next? Whatever happens, I feel ready for it.*'

'It will make you monstrously self-absorbed.'

Critics of journal writing – who often turn out to be skilful all-round critics – usually begin and end their criticism by rattling your fears that journal writing will make you more or even unbearably self-absorbed. So some warnings are in order.

It is true there will be times when you will want to write in your journal more than anything else. It is also true that there will be times when you may be thoroughly preoccupied with a most unexpected insight or revelation – especially one that comes to you like a brilliant flash after several weeks of ho-hum writing.

IT IS EVEN TRUE THAT YOU MIGHT COME TO THINK RATHER BETTER OF YOURSELF. ('Did *I* write that glorious sentence? Was it sensible, prosaic me who caught, perfectly, the bliss of stepping into an ocean pool on a hot summer's day? Is that really my own witty/wise/accurate insight? Am I the person who can make myself laugh a year after an event simply by reading what I wrote in such a rush?')

What is not true is that you will become more self-absorbed than you already are. Chances are good that you will become significantly *less* self-absorbed, *more interested* and certainly more interesting.

Generally speaking, we cling to our own view of things and to our own anxieties when we are unsure about ourselves. The more securely we trust the validity of our own existence, the easier it is to open up to the glories all around us.

YOU WILL CERTAINLY BECOME MUCH MORE CONFIDENT ABOUT WHAT YOU KNOW, THINK AND FEEL ABOUT YOUR OWN LIFE ONCE YOU START WRITING A JOURNAL.

Journal writing will have its many stages and phases. There will be self-absorbed periods. There will also be periods when your observations take you far from home – with one proviso: that these are your observations and no-one else's.

My view is that discovering what your observations are – rather than living second-hand – is one of the unrivalled joys of journal writing. If there have to be some moments of self-absorption to discover that, so be it.

JOURNAL WRITING CONNECTS US TO OUR DEEPEST SENSE OF SELF. It uncovers ourselves to ourselves. But the more deeply we delve, the less personal and more universal our discoveries will become.

AT THE PLACE OF OUR DEEPEST AND MOST AUTHENTIC EXPERIENCES, WE FEEL MOST ALIVE, EVEN IN TIMES OF SORROW.

Your journal writing will let you experience that. In fact, your journal writing will facilitate and accomplish that.

Anais Nin made an art form out of her journal writing. But she commented on it very simply: 'In the journal I am at ease.'

As you progress with your own journal writing, you will see for yourself how your moods and attitudes affect not only what you write, but also how you interpret what you have written. (Those variations alone will tell you a great deal about yourself.)

There will be times when you re-read something you regarded as unremarkable or dull, and find something in it that seems astonishingly helpful or new. Perhaps you now have the answer to an inner puzzle. Or can see how persistently you have been avoiding a key issue – or writing about it from a limited and unhelpful perspective only.

In all kinds of ways, journal writing will expand your choices, intensify your strengths and genuinely support you. But you do need to pay it regular attention! In this it is like any other intimate relationship. It gives back in direct proportion to what you bring to it. It certainly requires some commitment from you if it is to flourish. It also requires you to be truthful, and trusting of the writing process, even through flat or bleak periods. But in return, journal writing will give you a degree of clarity and insight that really does not come in any other way. (It offers something quite different from conversation, or from turning your thoughts over and over without 'getting them down' on paper.)

There is also something delightfully spontaneous and unstructured about journal writing. And I love that! There's no need to know exactly what you want to write about before starting (or to justify taking time for journal writing). In fact, the opposite is true. If you already knew just what you wanted to write, there would be no need to do so. Journal writing is not about 'getting the job done'. It's about understanding better your own precious and complex existence.

A sense of being increasingly in tune with your own existence is the unbeatable reward that journal writing offers. You will benefit, and so will everyone and everything that's in your life.

So let's get started.

'Daydreaming had started me on the way, but writing, once I was truly in its grip, took me and shook me awake.'

Eudora Welty

THE SEED OF THE INNER PERSON

'The seed of the inner person is the essence of a human being.
It carries the potentiality of life, and it is unique in each individual.
The urge to live is an affirmation of this seed, but its growth,
especially in its early stages, is soft and delicate. Like the young
shoot of a plant, its life is precarious. It is especially vulnerable to
the pressure and whims of the social environment. If it is to survive
it must build its own inner strength. It must be able to affirm
the private person within itself.'

Ira Progoff, At a Journal Workshop

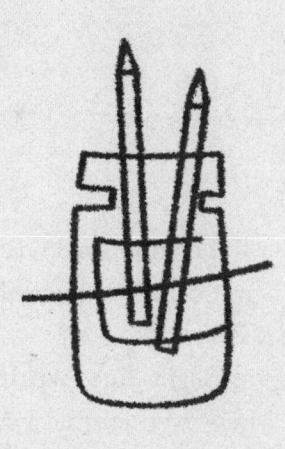

Getting Started

Start here. Or there.

There is no wrong reason to begin journal writing. Nor is there any wrong way to begin. When it comes to journal writing, there is *your* reason and *your* way. That's all.

You may want to go straight into writing about events and impressions. That's fine. However, journal writing can offer a rare chance to develop your creativity and to *pause*, fruitfully. In the next few chapters especially, that will be our focus.

Of course, your capacity to express yourself freely – to swim in the stream of your own creativity – may well have been sorely inhibited by the many years you spent at school. Forget school. However you write your journal is perfect. Whatever you write is perfect. Better still, however and whatever you write is beyond the reach of mundane judgements like 'perfect' or 'imperfect'. IT IS WHAT IT IS. Nothing more.

Let yourself off the hook, here in your own private journal at least. That will help you to become less judgemental of other people. It may also help you to be much less judgemental and much more supportive of yourself.

Some practical suggestions

* Write in your journal *regularly*. Even a few minutes' writing on a busy day makes a difference. It keeps you centred and it gives invaluable continuity to your discoveries.

* Keep your journal where no-one else will read it. You may want to share sections at some point. But don't do so too eagerly. This is, above everything, a process of self-discovery best done free even from the idea that someone else may be looking over your shoulder.

* Use a pen that flows smoothly and feels totally comfortable in your hand. Use several colours if you prefer. Free your creativity. ENJOY THE SENSUALITY OF MIND AND HAND USING PEN AND PAPER. (In this computer age, that is an increasingly rare treat.)

* Keep extra pages of high-quality thin paper that you can fold into this book. Many of the exercises you will want to do a number of times. Don't limit yourself to the number of blank pages that this journal offers.

* If you want to sketch or draw, or perhaps respond to an idea or situation by writing a short story or a poem, don't hesitate. 'Journal writing' includes and encourages every possible form of self-expression.

    Many literary writers have also been committed diary or journal writers. One of the most famous of these is Katherine Mansfield. In her diaries — parts of which were published after her death — there are drafts of letters, fragments of short stories, lots of ideas, inner arguments, sublime insights and the most mundane noting of events. ('J. went to town. I worked a little — chased the fowls.')

Jumping-off points: Getting started

* What are your instant associations with new beginnings? Write them down. Then explore them.
* Does this experience of journal writing feel in any way familiar? How?
* What 'new beginnings' do you recall from 5, 10, 15 years ago?
* Are you judging yourself already? Want to write about that?
* Fantasise about the word 'potential'. Write down everything it evokes and promises. Explore that.

Your turn

Make a list (in this journal) of what will support you in your journal writing. Start with what you need to buy. New pens? Additional paper? What kinds? Where will you go to get them? When?

Decide where you will sit to write your journal; how you will ensure quiet and privacy; what time of the day or evening will work best for you.

Let your instincts and imagination work together for you on this.

Visualise what you most want.

Write that down as a promise to yourself.

Use the jumping-off points above to stimulate your thinking and writing. Even at this planning stage don't forget to add detail to your writing. Describe where you are sitting and your state of mind. ('I am on the wooden bench in the garden today and am aware how lovely it is to look at the leaves for their own beauty rather than thinking about sweeping them up. That's what I need more time for: looking at leaves.')

Be aware of what's going on in your body. Describe it.

* A rhythm and routine for your
  journal writing honours the activity.
  It also keeps you on track.

* *Sit* somewhere that feels really
  good to you.

* Regard journal writing as a gift to
  yourself.

* Use *beautiful* paper for your extra
writing. Keep the pages in this
journal.

✳ Notice: You are already writing.

Liberate your curiosity

Your curiosity will be enhanced in countless ways by journal writing. Start by looking at it directly.

The people whose company you enjoy most, who seem most alive and wide awake, are also likely to be unashamedly curious and interested in all kinds of things. They don't want to know just how things happen, but why – and then what next? They want to dive into the richness of events; make sense of things; find and establish connections; enjoy it thoroughly when things don't immediately make sense. There is plenty of room for doubt in their minds. They can also allow their minds to be changed as new information comes towards them and meets new insights arising within them. They do not want to decide everything in advance. And they especially don't want 'everything' to be decided for them.

Writing about perhaps the most famous diarist of all, Samuel Pepys, Thomas Mallon says in *A Book of One's Own*:

'[Pepys] is blessed with a child's avidity for any
new piece of entertainment, science, invention,
fashion. He wants to know everything . . . He'll

discuss optics just after he's discussed teeth; go see an experiment in blood transfusion performed on a dog; marvel at a bearded lady; and wonder how this Italian sport of buggery he's heard about is actually performed . . . He is what the next century would call a great booby. And his willingness to be one so freely is his genius.'

Jumping-off points: Valuing curiosity

Who are the most curious, 'awake' and thoroughly alive people that you can think of? They could be people in your everyday life. Or people who live in your imagination: heroes, writers, characters in novels. You will understand them (and yourself) much better when you write about them. Focus especially on *your own connections to them*. ('Have always loved the way Ang pushes me to take risks as though it's the most natural thing in the world.')

* Choose instinctively. Don't worry if you 'should' be writing about this person or if that person is 'special' enough.
* The primary qualities you are searching out are 'curiosity' and 'aliveness'. They can manifest in all kinds of ways. Discover what each quality means to you: when you feel it most easily; if there are times when you don't feel it and would like to.
* Have you remembered some 'ordinary' people also?
* Did you include yourself? Or yourself as you are becoming?
* If you find this a tricky topic it makes it even more worthwhile to return to it a number of times, each time 'forgetting' everything you have already written and beginning afresh.
* Many children are taught to 'mind their own business', or to 'shut up and not ask questions'. Did that happen to you? How do you want to change that pattern now?
* Does your workplace invite a range of experience and opinion? Is it intellectually stimulating? Or stultifying? What do you want to do about it?

* Begin a list of ways to develop your capacity for curiosity. Journal writing will help.

Your turn

Start by noting the details of your surroundings. ('At home. Everyone else out. Sitting in red chair. Both cats asleep beside me.')

Describe how you feel about embarking on this exploration. (You will find that detail fascinating a few months from now.)

Begin to make your list of inspirational people.

Note the qualities you associate with each of them.

Explore your connections to them. ('His sense of humour reminds me of my boss . . .')

Look for what surprises you. Note that.

Use the jumping-off points above to keep you writing.

You may want to forget the inspirational people and go straight to writing about the qualities and your response to them. Follow that!

Write for at least 20 minutes at any one time.

Don't edit or rewrite.

If you feel stuck — just return to the idea of 'curiosity' or 'aliveness'. ('Funny that most of the people I admire for their aliveness are long dead . . .')

Notice and write about what's going on with your body. ('Started off feeling pretty tight and tense, that got worse for a bit, then felt like I was flying . . .')

This exercise is all about waking up your curiosity, so finish by completing this sentence: 'The most unexpected thing I have discovered today is . . .'

Don't re-read immediately.

Let your thoughts 'rest'.

✳ Explore *your* connections with the
people you admire. Write about
what they mean to *you* personally.

'I was a fantastic student until ten, and then my mind began to wander.'

Grace Paley

****

2   IDYLLES ET ÉLÉGIES

Sans prévenu, elle dit : « me voila
Ce cœur m'attend. Par l'Amour que
Comme autrefois j'y viens régner en
Au nom d'amour ma raison se troubl
Je voulus fuir, et tout mon corps tre
Je bégayai des plaintes au perfide.
Pour me toucher il prit un air timid
Puis à mes pieds, en pleurant, il ton

* The qualities you admire in others are the qualities that are germinating in you. Write about how you will cultivate them.

✳ Enjoy how *portable* your journal is.
You can write it in cafés, on the train,
late at night silently in your room.

* Keep your journal wrapped in a rich
piece of cloth. Honour the treasure
you are creating.

'There is in the British Museum an enormous mind. Consider that Plato is there cheek by jowl with Aristotle; and Shakespeare with Marlowe. This great mind is hoarded beyond the power of any single mind to possess it.'

Virginia Woolf

27

✳ Envisage a situation where you need
  the quality you admire. Write about
  the situation as though the quality
  is fully developed in you.

✳ Humility should not be confused
  with a sense of unworthiness.
  One keeps us real; the other keeps
  us small.

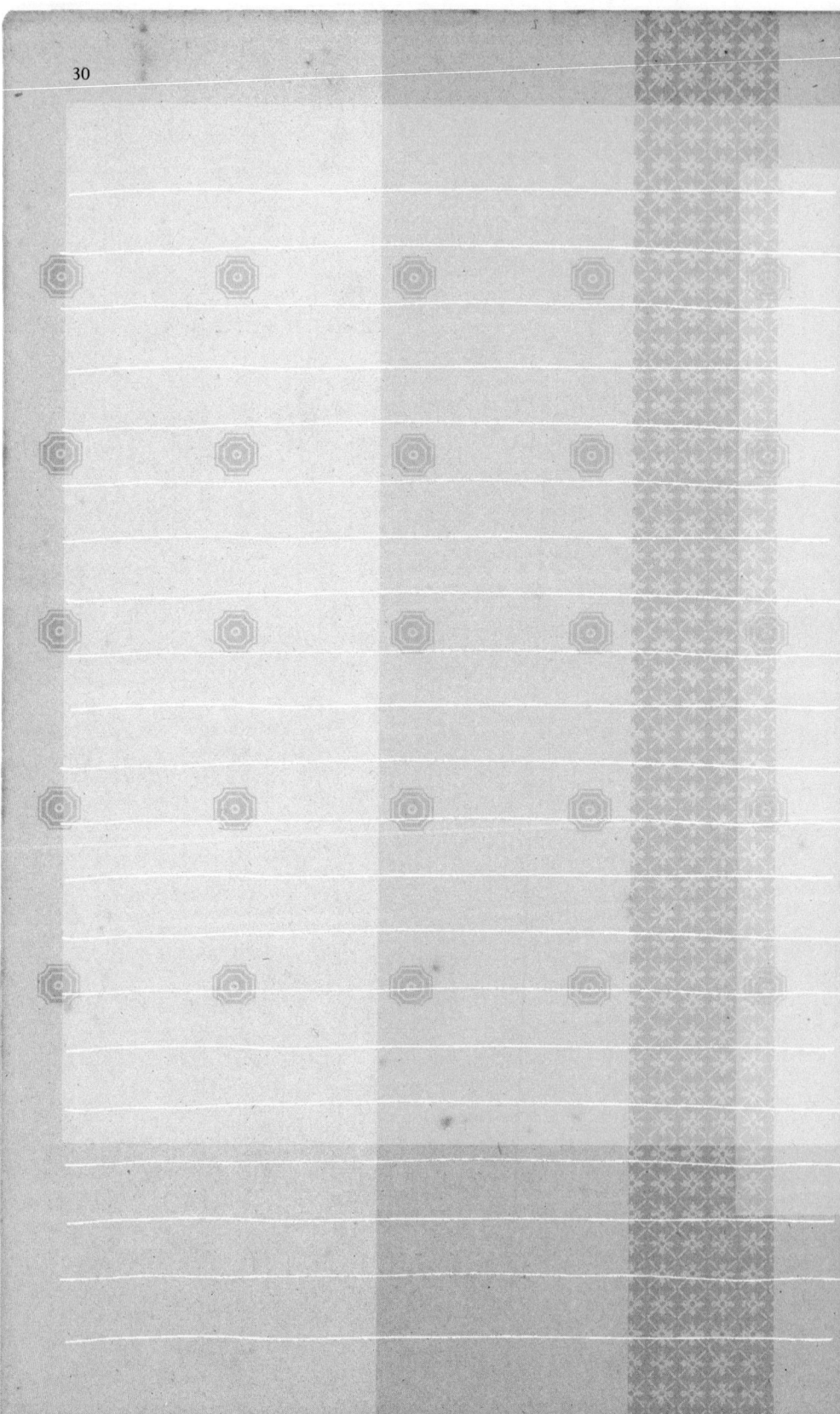

✳ We each have the seeds for all
the human qualities within us.
We need only 'water' them with
our attention.

✳ Don't be ashamed if you envy
others. That also tells you what you
need to 'wake up' in yourself.
Write about that.

'If only one could have two lives, the first in which to make one's mistakes ... and the second in which to profit by them.'

D. H. Lawrence

* Do you feel closer to those qualities
now than when you began thinking
about them?
Which quality is most special to you?

'We all live with the objective of being happy; our lives are different and yet the same.'

Anne Frank

Journal writing and you

Liberate your curiosity about journal writing itself. Begin by writing about your motivations, hopes and dreams for this journal: *your* journal.

What are *you* prepared to give to your journal?

What do you want it to give you?

What would make journal writing 'worthwhile'?

Jumping-off points: Journal writing

* If you bought this journal yourself, what was running through your mind at that moment of choice and purchase?
* If someone else gave it to you, what did you feel at the moment of receiving it?
* What are your associations with journal writing – the words that most quickly spring to mind?
* What are your associations with journal *writers* – again, the words that most quickly spring to mind?
* Are those ideas first or second-hand (your own or your parents', teachers', your ex-lover's ideas)?
* What published journals, if any, have inspired you?

* What areas of your life most urgently need your attention? (Who says so?)
* Are there any particular emotions that you want to explore? Are there any situations where you feel stuck or even hopeless?
* What talents do you have that journal writing might support you to develop?

The points given above are prompts only. You don't need to answer each of them. Or any of them. Let yourself respond to them instinctively. Let yourself be 'grabbed' by one of them.

YOU MAY WANT TO RETURN TO THE SAME QUESTION FOR DAYS ON END. That's always a sign there's lots going on in your unconscious.

Also, remember that whatever the 'topic', it is allowing you to think more broadly and generally about all kinds of issues. You may start with one topic, for example, and find yourself writing about something quite different. Trust that!

In my own writing I rarely know whether a specific item that interests me is a 'clue' about something else or is fascinating in its own right. But that's what's so marvellous about writing, especially when you allow yourself 'to be written'. It never ceases to be surprising.

Your turn

Make yourself comfortable.

Turn off all distractions (phone, television, radio).

Begin by noting details of where and when you are writing. ('I am sitting in the airport lounge waiting to fly to Sydney. The plane's late, but who cares . . .')

Start with this phrase: 'I am writing this journal because . . .'

Use the jumping-off points above whenever you need to.

If you slow down at any time or feel stuck, just return to this same phrase: 'I am writing this journal because . . .'

It is also productive to comment on your immediate state of mind. ('I notice that I am finding it hard to stop worrying whether I am doing this right . . .' 'I feel excited, like the time when I . . .' 'I don't really care why I am writing this journal, all I know is . . .')

Notice if your state of mind changes. Write about that. ('I'm not feeling so strung out any more, even though I'm finding it quite hard to get going in my journal today . . .')

Write for at least 20 minutes.

Don't edit or rewrite.

Be aware of what's going on in your body as well as your emotions.

When you feel finished, complete this sentence: 'What I discovered today is . . .'

Don't re-read immediately.

Let your thoughts 'rest'.

You are becoming a monitor, an observer of your own inner world. And your outer world. Perceive how inner and outer are in a constant state of interconnection and interdependence. Value that.

'Playing so many roles . . . I had to find one place of truth, one dialogue without falsity. This is the role of the diary.'

Anais Nin

* Look at your handwriting. Does it
tell a story? Is it more energetic and
rapid in some parts than others?
What are your associations with
handwriting?

✱ Are you enraged or amused by
any of the directions or prompts?
Worth exploring? Argue here,
in the journal.

✱ How familiar are the reactions you
are expressing? Are you caught in
a spiral? *Write* your way out.

'The habits of a lifetime when everything else had to come before writing are not easily broken.'

Tillie Olson

_____

_____

_____

_____

_____

_____

_____

_____

_____

_____

_____

_____

_____

_____

_____

_____

_____

_____

* Notice which insights especially
interest or surprise you. Write more
about those?

* What feels fresh here? (Does *fresh*
matter?)

_____

_____

_____

_____

'All good writing is swimming under water and holding your breath.'

F. Scott Fitzgerald

IDYLLES ET ÉLÉGIES

Sans prevenu, elle dit ... me voila
Ce cœur m'attend. Par l'Amour que
Comme autrefois j'y viens régner en
Au nom d'amour ma raison se troubl
Je voulus fuir, et tout mon corps tre
Je bégayai des plaintes au perfide.
Pour me toucher il prit un air timid
Puis à mes pieds, en pleurant, il ton

* Check out the jumping-off points again (see pages 36–37). Different ones may now interest you.

* What have you not yet thought or written? (Close your eyes. *Let yourself 'see' this imaginatively.*)

Deepen your self-awareness

We often feel hurt or insulted when someone misreads us or behaves towards us in ways that we believe are insensitive or outdated. Yet sometimes we are also slow to catch up with how we have developed, or what our current attitudes and interests really are. Journal writing is a wonderful way to stay in tune with your life right now.

As you continue your journal writing, *simply return to this same theme*. ('Journal writing and me.' 'How I feel about committing myself to this enterprise.' 'What I am wanting from it.' 'Why this is the moment for self-discovery.' 'How I hope it will develop my creativity.')

You might do this for a number of weeks. There is no limit. Journal writing is about process, not outcome. It is totally free of 'productivity' demands. Relish that. And write about it.

Some practical suggestions

* Write about the novelty of returning to the same topic repeatedly, trusting there is more to know.
* Writing about journal writing, you are giving yourself a chance

to see how you view your own inner world and everyone around you.

* Push through your own boredom. Often insight is directly on the other side.
* When you feel 'stuck', describe that state of mind in your journal. Be a scientific observer of your own condition. ('I kept writing in circles, just commenting on that, then suddenly I took off against all my own expectations . . .')
* Go against the current tide that tells you 'instant is best'. That's only sometimes true in journal writing. Here you can be a tortoise *and* a hare.
* 'Forget' what you wrote yesterday. Practise coming into *this* day, freshly.
* Are your expectations high enough?
* Notice whether you have been concentrating mostly on 'thoughts'. If so, look at the *feelings* associated with journal writing.
* If you have written a lot about your feelings, take some time to review your *thoughts*. Or look at these feelings themselves somewhat dispassionately. What do you think about those feelings? What conclusions are you jumping to?
* Notice with interest where you might be limiting yourself.
* Ask yourself what you are avoiding. (Write down the question. Write down your answer. It is *all* journal fodder.)
* Notice with interest what's exciting you.
* Notice with interest what else you are dying to be writing about! (Make notes. Promise yourself that it won't be long.)

Your turn

Use the prompts above to deepen your knowledge not just about journal writing but about your relationship to your own unique inner world.

Each day, note the time, date and place of your writing.

You might also want to note your own sense of anticipation.

What do you want to discover today?

How impatient do you feel about 'not moving on'?

How relieved do you feel that there is no rush or pressure?

Give yourself time to reflect on your topic as though you had never come to it before.

Then let yourself write instinctively and freely.

Write for at least 20 minutes.

Don't edit or rewrite.

If you suddenly find you are writing about 'something else', go with that. ('I got to writing about how hard it is for me to know what I want for myself, how out of practice I am at standing up for what I want . . .')

Be aware of what's going on in your body — and write about that.

If you notice strong emotions or associations arising as you write, include them in your writing.

When you feel 'written out', complete this sentence: 'It's good to have discovered . . .' Or: 'What I want to know more about is . . .'

Don't re-read immediately.

Let your thoughts 'rest'.

✳ Write a string of adjectives to
describe this inner voyage: 'scary,
exhilarating, unknown'. Keep adding
to the list. Enjoy the poetry trail you
are creating.

✳ Experiment with writing more
directly: 'Dear Journal . . .'. Anne
Frank addressed her journal as
'Dear Kitty'.

* Try writing in the third person:
'Andrea Brown has never done this
kind of thing before . . .'

* Review how often you are writing
'I think . . .' Switch to 'I feel'. Or vice
versa.

'We don't see things as they are, we see things as we are.'

Anais Nin

'We want the answers, when the questions themselves are more engaging . . . The question takes on new shades of meaning as we peel away the layers of ourselves.'

Ellen Sue Stern

✳ Choose extra pages to write on and
keep them in or with this journal.

Where home is

'Home' and 'self' are two of the most powerful words in any language. Explore the idea of home *as a way of understanding yourself better*.

Some practical suggestions

* For several weeks, use the word 'home' as your key prompt.
* Start with any of the sentences that follow – or create your own.
* Note the time, date and place of your writing.
* Be aware that 'home' is a very potent word. Go slowly if you know there are painful associations for you. Don't force anything.
* You may want to draw sometimes rather than write. That can also give you great insights and release. If you are used to thinking verbally, drawing can be especially helpful. It truly does not matter if you are good at drawing or not. The idea is to think in images and get those down.
* You can also add photos or gather up postcards of paintings that show exteriors or interiors of homes. What you are searching

for is not so much the outer forms as atmosphere, associations and subtle resonances of personal meaning.

* Whenever you return to this topic, try to set aside what you have already thought and written. Come to it with a 'beginner's mind' — as though for the first time. You will be delighted by how productive that can be.

Your turn

Describe your inner state as you begin to write. ('I feel like I should be doing the accounts so that's a bit of a familiar struggle.')

Then respond freely to any one of these prompts:

'My first home was . . .'

'What I value most about my current home is . . .'

'I feel as though I am missing . . .'

'My ideal home is . . .'

'What makes a feeling of home for me is . . .'

'I feel "at home" when . . .'

'When I think about home I remember . . .'

'The smells of home for me are . . .'

'People matter more to me than place . . .'

'The most important room for me in any house is . . .'

'I could only write this journal at home because . . .'

'For me home is not a place at all . . .'

'My idea of "home" changed when . . .'

'The objects in my current home I'd rescue first are . . .'

'The idea of "home" for me extends way beyond four walls . . .'

Choose one prompt only at a time. Let yourself go into it deeply.

Give yourself time to reflect on it before writing.

Once you begin, let yourself write instinctively and without 'rules'.

You may want to start simply by writing all your associations with the word and idea and emotions of 'home'.

Write for at least 20 minutes.

Don't edit or rewrite.

Be aware of what's going on in your body. Describe that.

If you notice strong emotions or associations arising as you write, include them in your writing. ('It's funny but as I write about home I am feeling really frustrated with myself that I don't invite people here more often – that somehow I've got out of the way of . . .' 'I remember making sets of cushions when I was first married. Fat cushions stuffed with hope.')

If you feel stuck, begin again with whichever prompt you chose as your opener: 'The smells of home for me are . . .'.

Notice if there have been any shifts in the way you think about home – or yourself.

At the end of your journal entry, complete this sentence: ' My deepest idea about home seems to be . . .'

Don't re-read immediately.

Let your thoughts 'rest'.

'Home is the place where, when you have to go there /
They have to take you in . . .'

Robert Frost

* 'Free associate' with the idea of home.
  List all your associations with home,
  then circle those that interest you most.

'This is my city, the hills and harbour water / I call home . . .'

Lauris Edmond

'Swimming at a depth of thirty meters, I once entered a cave through a low, narrow opening . . . It was there I found my God.'

Enzo Maiorca

* Describe your current home from the point of view of someone else.

IDYLLES ET ÉLÉGIES

Sans prevenir, elle dit : « Me voila.
Ce cœur m'attend. Par l'Amour que
Comme autrefois j'y viens régner en
Au nom d'amour ma raison se troubl
Je voulus fuir, et tout mon corps tre
Je bégayai des plaintes au perfide.
Pour me toucher il prit un air timide
Puis à mes pieds, en pleurant, il to

✻ Note which of your insights surprises
you or makes your spirits lift.

✻ Review how often you are writing
'I think…'. Switch to 'I feel'. Or vice versa.

* What does your home 'need'?

* Let your home write a letter to you.
  ('Dear Jenny, I love the way you put
  on wild music whenever you dust
  me...')

'Opening the window, I open myself.'

Natalya Gorbanevskaya

* Ask someone close to you what their
idea of home is.

* Find a piece of writing that expresses
'home' for you. Or a piece of music.
Or make a special dish or recipe that
conjures up home. Write about that
experience.

A source of freedom

Writing a journal is a way of honouring your own life that also brings invaluable freedoms.

* Freedom to know your own mind(s) – both conscious and unconscious.
* Freedom to see what drives you.
* Freedom to know what supports you.
* Freedom to be creative (in your own way).
* Freedom to understand yourself as well as others.
* Freedom to make good use of your own insights.
* Freedom to see what really matters to you.
* Freedom to make mistakes. (How else can you learn?)
* Freedom to stop repeating your mistakes!
* Freedom to discover what you need to do about challenging situations.
* Freedom to live at the centre of your own life – while becoming *less* self-centred.
* Freedom to observe your own life unfolding.
* Freedom to care about the lives of others.
* Freedom to extend your creativity to every corner of your life.

In the West we generally take the idea of 'freedom' as a given. Yet how can we treasure it fully if we don't truly understand what freedoms matter to us — and why?

It's good to explore this topic not from an abstract point of view, but by discovering how it is experienced and lived out in your everyday life. What you are really discovering is more about yourself. Freedom is the vehicle; it's an exhilarating one.

Your turn

Note the details of where and when you are writing.

Note your state of mind — right now. ('Wondering if I have anything to say . . .')

Take a few moments to reflect on which of the freedoms listed above are most important to you.

Choose instinctively.

Note them down.

Choose just one to write about. (You can come back to the others.)

Be sure to note down the emotions, thoughts and hopes that arise with your choice. ('Most of all I want to find out why Mum said we could choose our own careers but then . . .')

Note all your associations with your topic — however indirect.

If you had more of this freedom, what would that give you? How would your life be different? Would the way you see yourself be any different?

You don't need to write anything 'important' just because this is an important topic. Above all, it is a self-discovery exercise: start and finish with whatever comes to the forefront of your mind.

You don't even need to write complete sentences. You may want to start by 'free associating': allowing a string of words to jump from your mind onto the page. ('Free to understand myself . . . no-one coming into my room without

knocking . . . including the "rooms" of my mind . . . KEEP OUT . . .')
Be aware of what's going on in your body as well as your feelings. ('I feel like
a mountain goat, nimble and light-footed . . .')
Write for at least 20 minutes.
Don't edit or rewrite.
Finish by completing this sentence: 'Today I have discovered . . .'
Don't re-read immediately.
Let your thoughts 'rest'.

'I want to write, but more than that, I want to bring out all kinds of things
that lie buried deep in my heart.'

Anne Frank

* Choose beautiful paper for extra writing. Keep those pages in or with this journal.

* What does the idea of a 'free spirit' mean to you?

'When we can't dream any longer, we die.'

Emma Goldman

69

✳ Have fun 'free associating' in
relation to freedom: let a string of
words jump from your mind onto
the page. Don't censor.

✳ Check: am I writing *freely*?

* A 'conversation' is a great thing to
have on paper. If you are arguing out
an idea in your mind, *write it down
from perspective A and also
perspective B.*

* Some inner boundaries are really vital.
Which ones matter most to you?

'I have just re-read my year's diary and am much struck by the rapid haphazard gallop at which it swings along . . . if I stopped and took thought, it would never be written at all.'

Virginia Woolf

IDYLLES ET ÉLÉGIES

Sans prévenir, elle dit : « Me voilà !
Ce cœur m'attend. Par l'Amour que
Comme autrefois j'y viens régner enc
Au nom d'amour ma raison se troubl
Je voulus fuir, et tout mon corps tre
Je bégayai des plaintes au perfide.
Pour me toucher il prit un air timid
Puis à mes pieds, en pleurant, il tom

'I always write in my diary when we quarrel.'

Sophie Tolstoy

LADEN WITH TREASURES . . .

'To write is to sit and stare, hypnotized, at the reflection of the window in the silver inkstand, to feel the divine fever mounting to one's cheeks and forehead while the hand that writes grows blissfully numb upon the paper. It also means idle hours curled up in the hollow of the divan, and then an orgy of inspiration, from which one emerges stupefied and aching all over, but already recompensed, and laden with treasures that one unloads slowly onto the virgin page in the little round pool of light under the lamp.'

Colette, The Vagabond

How to Write

Already writing

You are, I suspect, already writing! There may be pages of writing in this journal that testify to that. What I'm offering now are ideas to help you to write your journal more freely and enjoyably, but *in your own way*.

These hints are designed to give you confidence and broaden your range. If you have studied literary writing, or are used to writing academic essays or business reports, you may need these hints rather more than those whose writing education has been more slap-dash. This is because you may have to wean yourself from the habit of writing to impress — or compete. You will also have to wean yourself from the notion that there is an ideal way to do things. Or one that is most effective. (There isn't.) It's fine, of course, to want to impress yourself when writing your journal. But other things are even more important.

There will be days when you open your journal and find that it writes itself. Leslie describes that.

> **LESLIE**
>
> 'I started off by recording whatever event in the day felt most unfinished. I could have chosen what was most interesting or surprising or maybe complicated. But for me "unfinished" was the thing most likely to keep me awake at night and make me feel small or helpless. What I would always find, though, is that one thing led to another. I might start with a problem from work, for example, and then find I was writing about something I remembered from another situation entirely.
>
> 'I love the times when the writing flows like that and makes its own jumps from one thing to another. It's always unpredictable why it will do that. It's not about being tired or having more energy. It just happens.'

There may be other times when you feel you need a routine to call on – either to get started or to sustain you. This is often true when you are entering difficult new emotional terrain. Perhaps you are allowing yourself to be more honest than you have been previously. (Journal writing will make you more honest. From that flows a healing sense of integrity and wholeness about your entire life.)

Perhaps you are working with tough issues, like forgiveness. Or it may be that your self-confidence is low and you feel that you have only your commitment to your journal to sustain you.

I know that I often feel astonishingly physically restless when my mind is reaching towards something, but I am not quite 'there'. Or when I am about to write something that is emotionally challenging and I feel shaky or uncertain. At those times I pace my office, taking books off my shelves and reading brief snatches of other people's writing before my mind darts on to something else. Or I leave my office altogether and go for long, speedy walks. Or I drift around clothes shops or art galleries in a kind of daze while some part of my mind continues to work on what is actually engaging me. In those strange, restless times I am also likely to feel extremely hungry, literally needing something tough or crunchy to 'get my teeth into'.

Writing a journal, it is possible to incorporate all of those observations. ('I want to be writing about going to see Gran and Pop, but something's getting in the way and after three cups of coffee I feel like I am spinning off the planet, which reminds me of the time when . . .')

Observing what is going on in the present moment (and not just what happened earlier in the day or week) is integral to journal writing. What's more, it can be far more direct and even more truthful than recording experiences that have already had time to settle.

Curiosity is key here. Observe whatever is happening with interest. You are observing to find out more and not to judge or criticise.

Keeping to your routine of writing, and observing *the process of writing* with as much interest as the content of your days, gives you an invaluable sense of inner stability — even at times of uncertainty.

This was Helena's experience.

HELENA

'My promise to myself was to write in my journal at least every second day. I wrote that promise into the front of my journal and I've kept to it, too, except on a couple of occasions. Some days I just make a note of what is strongest in my mind. More often, though, I try to develop at least one issue further by writing for half an hour or so. If I have real difficulties with it, then I take it as a signal that this is a knotty issue for me. That is, when I am slowed up, I know there will be a reason for that – so I investigate what's going on. I ask myself questions like, "Is this familiar?" or "How would this look a month or a year from now?" Or I might just jot down all the feelings and associations I have with the particular issue. Then I often leave it to "brew". I have told my subconscious that I'm interested, then I wait for a response. Sometimes I have to wait a while, but there will always come a dream, or a rush of writing, or just a sudden insight, that gives me more information than diligent, linear writing ever could.'

Free writing

As much as possible, when you are writing in this journal or on the pages you are adding to it, write freely.

What do I mean by this?

Some practical suggestions

* Relax and make yourself physically comfortable. That will also help settle your mind.
* Have everything you need to hand.
* Turn off all distractions (phone, television, radio).
* Decide what you are going to write about. (This journal offers many suggestions.)
* Let yourself soak into your topic by holding it in your thoughts. *Drift* with it.
* When you feel ready, begin to write. As you will already have noticed, I often give a prompt or a sentence with which you can start and to which you can return when you hesitate or run out of steam. Similar prompts are given in the summary section of this journal (see pages 213–216). They are literally keys, undoing the locks in your mind and freeing up all kinds of associations.

* *Keep writing for at least 20 minutes.* This is perhaps most important of all. If you give up too soon, you will soon believe that you have nothing to discover.
* Push through your boredom or sense of irritation with yourself by including your observations of that in your writing. ('God help me, I seem to be writing about my horrible job yet again . . . so maybe it is time to do something about it, but today I had thought I was writing about home, so why is it that I can never feel "at home" in any workplace when I give work all that time and attention?')
* Don't stop to edit or rewrite.
* Notice what is happening in your body. Write about that.
* What you write does not have to be deep and meaningful. Judging yourself in that way gets in the way of writing freely. Journal writing is *for you*.

Sometimes you will be writing about the same topic for several weeks. As your confidence develops, you may find that you are keeping several 'strands' of journal writing going simultaneously. You may, for example, return to the theme of 'home' quite consistently while also tracking on a daily basis what's going on for you personally, as well as occasionally dropping in a comment about a book you have read, a dinner you have cooked, a play you have seen or a novel you plan to write!

Journal writing is, above everything, freeing. There are no rules. Enjoy that.

CAREY

'As a lawyer, I have to be super-organised. I thought that I would write my journal in the same kind of way, but actually if I look at it now, a year later, it's a riot! I write with different coloured pens according to my mood. I print some sections and handwrite others. I draw in odd corners. I do follow themes through, but I am also always going back to things that I half-thought I had finished with. I see journal writing as an anti-linear process, which is pretty radical for me. That certainly makes it far more enjoyable than I expected. It's as far from my experience of study and work as it could possibly be.'

'By keeping a diary of what made me happy I had discovered that happiness came when I was most widely aware.'

Joanna Field

Your life in your journal

Journal writing takes you way beyond the mere recording of facts. ('Went to Newcastle. Saw Tom.') Facts can be a useful prompt for future writing or reflecting. And at times when you have barely combed your hair or flossed your teeth for several days then perhaps a few 'facts' may be all that you can manage in your journal writing. But more usually, regard the facts as your diving board and the world of impressions as the bottomless pool into which you can, at any time, fearlessly dive.

Some practical suggestions

* Develop the habit of recording events in your life as they occur.
* Spend *at least* as much time recording your *impressions*. These are often more important than the events themselves. Don't censor them. ('Went to Newcastle fairly reluctantly. Sense of duty probably. But when I saw Tom it was really clear to me that . . .')
* Take an interest in your life! If you don't, who will?
* Experience what it's like to look into your life as an observer.

What kind of observer are you? (Observe the observer!)
Be frank about what you find. Be outrageously curious.

* Know that we choose with our conscious minds. *But in writing,
  our unconscious mind can quickly take over.* That's one of the
  greatest possible rewards of journal writing. It takes you
  beneath the surface so fast – to the deepest reaches of
  existence.

Start and finish with the details

On 5 November 1936, Virginia Woolf, having just finished her novel
The Years, wrote these lines in her journal (published as *A Writer's
Diary*):

'The miracle is accomplished. L. [Virginia's
husband, Leonard] put down the last sheet about
12 last night; and could not speak. He was in tears.
He says it is 'a most remarkable book' – he *likes*
it better than *The Waves* – and has not a spark of
doubt that it must be published. I, as a witness,
not only to his emotion but to his absorption,
for he read on and on, can't doubt his opinion.
What about my own? Anyhow the moment of
relief was divine. I hardly know yet if I'm on my
heels or head, so amazing is the reversal since
Tuesday morning. I have never had such an
experience before.'

In *Writing Down the Bones*, Natalie Goldberg fine-tunes the details
wonderfully of a highly subjective viewpoint and account:

'Be awake to the details around you, but don't be
self-conscious. "Okay. I'm at a wedding. The bride
has on blue. The groom is wearing a red carnation.

They are serving chopped liver on doilies." Relax, enjoy the wedding, be present with an open heart. You will naturally take in your environment, and later, sitting at your desk, you will be able to recall just how it was dancing with the bride's redheaded mother, seeing the bit of red lipstick smeared on her front tooth when she smiled, and smelling her perfume mixed with perspiration.'

The details of a situation will always come into your mind with far greater clarity when you tune into them via your physical senses.

How did your body feel as you sat through the meeting? What was it like to be touched (physically or emotionally) at the gathering after the baby's christening? What was the physical environment like when you went to enquire about the new job? What were your feelings as you went up the stairs to the building? What kind of environment would you name as 'ideal'? Do you know what you are looking for — or want? How did the place smell? Did it 'feel' safe and friendly? What was the person's quality of voice? How did you react to that? (Do you know how your own voice sounds to others?)

Recording these details does far more than enliven your journal writing. It trains you to observe even the most unpromising situations with far greater interest and subtlety. Waiting for a friend, for example, on a busy city corner, could be an experience of total frustration. ('Where is she? How dare she be late?') Equally, it could be an exercise in observation: of the people rushing by you, the heat from the road, the loneliness of someone sitting at the bus-stop opposite, the crazy number of fast-food outlets, the absence of organic groceries . . . It could also be an invaluable exercise in self-awareness. ('I felt really impatient and upset first off. Then I decided to forget Carol entirely and just notice that if I relaxed my body and especially my knees a bit my mind could also go down into first gear and I could chill completely without much effort. So it was actually a bit of a jolt when she arrived, totally flustered because her bus had broken down . . .')

It's all in the details (and attitude)!

Your turn

Relax your body and mind.

Note where and when you are writing. ('At my desk. A quiet moment, remarkably . . .')

Start with this prompt: 'Today I am choosing to write about. . . .'

The issue of choice is crucial here. Each day presents you with a thousand things you could write about. But your mind flies to one topic rather than to another. Speculating about this process is part of journal writing. ('Here I am, worrying again about writing to Alice.')

Also, you (and I) make many decisions unconsciously. Until you learn to choose consciously, your life will feel as though it is in other people's hands. Consciously choosing engages your will, as well as your mind and heart. It brings you into the centre of your own existence.

Be ready to take off in another direction at any time. ('I thought I was choosing to write about my fears of getting old and suddenly I was writing about my darling school friend Julie . . .')

You don't need to write anything 'important'.

You don't even need to write whole sentences.

Tune into the details via all your senses: touch the situation; smell, taste, hear and feel it. Note what doing that is like.

Write for at least 20 minutes.

Don't stop to edit or rewrite.

Finish by completing this sentence: 'My strongest impression today is . . .'

Don't re-read immediately.

Let your thoughts 'rest'.

Each day return to the same opening phrase: 'Today I am choosing to write about . . .'

Finish with the same closing phrase: 'My strongest impression today is . . .'

✳ What does the idea of 'choice' mean
   to you?
   Do you exercise choice consciously?
   'Free associate': write down a string of
   ideas about choice without censoring.

'Writing in your journal gives you a chance to go back over your day and extract meaning from a hurried meeting with a friend or retrieve the significance of some fleeting event.'

Janette Rainwater

* Do you ever say or feel that other
  people are 'choosing' for you?
  Write about that.

'More than a week has passed, but I can't remember how.'

Evelyn Waugh

✳ Who or what are you *avoiding* in your journal writing?

✳ Would you be writing differently if you were confident no-one would ever read this?

✳ Write about a complex event in the third person: 'Jane was the only person in the room who...'

✳ Write to *yourself* from the point of view of an antagonist or rival: 'Dear Justine...'

_____

_____

_____

_____

_____

_____

_____

_____

_____

_____

_____

_____

_____

_____

_____

_____

_____

*   Are you self-justifying? Or self-criticising? Is that an old habit? Time to move on?

*   What senses are you using and describing: taste, feel, touch, smell, hearing?

'Truth is such a rare thing, it is delightful to tell it.'

Emily Dickinson

'How do I know what I think, until I see what I say?'

W. H. Auden

✳ Are you *enjoying* yourself, right now?
Is your 'mood' a matter of choice?

* Be alert to the *patterns* that are emerging.

Recording impressions and events

Conventional journal or diary writing usually primarily involves recording events. As your familiarity with journal writing deepens, you will quite naturally develop the capacity to observe yourself somewhat dispassionately; to look at events and interactions from other people's points of view; to discover the emotions that are driving different situations; to see the patterns in your own emotional habits and reactions. That kind of straightforward journal writing has tremendous value.

In her novel *Fear of Flying*, Erica Jong's heroine, Isadora Wing, reflects on what journal writing has given her:

> 'As I read the notebook, I began to be drawn into it as into a novel. I almost began to forget that I had written it. And then a curious revelation started to dawn. I stopped blaming myself; it was that simple . . . [It was] heartening to see how much I had changed in the past four years.'

If recording impressions and events is your primary motivation for keeping a journal, then keep the following practical suggestions in mind – and refer to them often. (If recording impressions and events is *not* your primary motivation for keeping a journal, you may nevertheless want to incorporate some element of this, not least to get a stronger sense of the continuity and unfolding of events in your life, and especially to become more accurately aware of where, why, how you feel 'in charge' or 'swept away' or 'taken over'.)

Some practical suggestions

* Keep in mind that change is inevitable. Writing about and understanding change, and your attitudes to it, gives invaluable strength to your life.
* Notice which events consistently clamour for your attention. What's going on? And what is *not* going on?
* Give yourself regular opportunities to review what you are *never* writing about. (How come you are always writing about the people who cause you grief, but never those who support or delight you?)
* Date your entries. Also note the time of day you are writing. You may be surprised how differently you see things mid-week, or maybe late at night.
* Note where you are writing, even the circumstances – especially when you are away from home. ('Taking precious time between meetings . . .')
* *Before* you launch into a description of the meeting that went terribly wrong or wonderfully well, ask yourself, 'How am I now, right at this minute?' *Record your answer.* ('Tonight I feel exhausted but agitated.' 'Today I feel rather slow and dreamy.')
* Occasionally sit back at the end of your writing and ask yourself, 'What did I discover today?' Take your time with this and if possible repeat it several times, writing down your answer and then returning to your same question, 'What did

I discover today?'. (This question may refer to your day, or to your journal writing.) Allow yourself to be surprised.

* Observe the difference between recording an event and an impression of that same event. (More about this in the previous chapter.)
* Notice that impressions can be passionate and dispassionate.
* Sometimes ask, 'How has my mood changed since I began to write today?' Occasionally there will be stark changes. At other times the change will be subtle. Either way is just fine.
* Record your impressions of new people and new situations. This will help you hone your instincts – especially when you are good-humoured enough to recognise how wrong you can sometimes be!
* Record your assumptions about how new people might be seeing you. Look for patterns.
* Once a month or so – not more often – read back over your entries. Look for patterns in both events and your impressions of them. Are you consistently being the brave martyr? Or worrying too much about what others think? Are you being truthful? In all areas of your life, are you being faithful to your highest values? Are you 'owning up' to your part in things? Are you taking time to notice what is fruitful and rewarding? Are you satisfied with the direction of your journal writing – and the life your journal is reflecting?

An invaluable opportunity to be yourself

Honing your insights and instincts, and setting down your thoughts on the page, you will feel more balanced and grounded in your everyday life. You will feel more entitled to your opinions and less defensive of them. You will be able to take knocks and disappointments more easily. (And gain insights from them.) You will be able to appreciate the good moments with increased ease and trust. You will have more to think about. Without even trying, you will feel more alive.

Your turn

Use any of the practical suggestions on the previous pages, or any of the margin notes that follow, as prompts to deepen your knowledge of how you respond to events and form impressions.

Choose one detail to concentrate on and develop. Write down what that is. ('Want to think about change and my responses to it over the last year.')

Give yourself time to reflect on your topic.

Incorporate those reflections in your writing.

Note where and when you are writing. ('In the car outside the dentist . . .')

Note your hopes for this topic. ('No idea what I want at this point . . .')

Be aware of what's going on in your body. Write about that.

If you notice strong emotions or associations arising as you write, include them in your writing.

Write instinctively and freely.

Write for at least 20 minutes.

Don't stop to edit or rewrite.

At the end of your journal entry, complete this sentence: 'Interested to notice that . . .'

Don't re-read immediately.

Let your thoughts 'rest'.

'What you know in your head will not sustain you in moments of crisis . . . confidence comes from body awareness, knowing what you feel in the moment.'

Marion Woodman

'I want, by understanding myself, to understand others.'

Katherine Mansfield

103

* Note five events that happened
  before you left the house today.

* Getting dressed today, what did you
  want your clothes to express?

✳ When did you last meet
   someone new? What did you think
   of them? What did they think of
   you? Does this fit a pattern?

✳ What would you most like someone
   new to notice about you?

'I got up at 5 and went to get water.'

Carolina Maria de Jesus

* How do you feel, right at this moment?

* What matters to you most, right at
  this moment?

'Lovely night, warm, and filled with gentle summer noises. I don't feel like writing ... Instead I am going to listen to the whispering trees.'

Edda Walker

* Look at an important event in your
  life through the eyes of someone
  you admire. Write about it from their
  perspective.

* Look at an important event in your
  present life from five years in the future.

✳ What would it mean to accept
someone at face value?

IDYLLES ET ÉLÉGIES

Sans prévenir, elle dit : « me voilà.
Ce cœur m'attend. Par l'Amour que
Comme autrefois j'y viens régner enc
Au nom d'amour ma raison se troubl
Je voulus fuir, et tout mon corps tre
Je bégayai des plaintes au perfide.
Pour me toucher il prit un air timid
Puis à mes pieds, en pleurant, il tor

* Think of someone close to you.
Write a description of their state of
mind right at this moment. Are you
surprised?

'I don't care about posterity. I am writing for today.'

Kurt Weill

Reviewing the process

From time to time, when you are in a comfortable, expansive frame of mind, review your journal writing. Do this *not* to criticise it, but to discover more about the processes of your inner world and state of mind and feelings – and more about the process of journal writing itself.

Jumping-off points: Reviewing your writing

* Are you focusing on one area of your life only?
* Are you writing about positive events as well as painful ones?
* Can you shift perspective by describing an event from someone else's point of view? ('When I wrote about our fight from Kate's point of view it made me much less tense . . . I knew I was fighting about nothing much.')
* What emotions or attitudes is your journal writing supporting and enhancing? (That choice is entirely up to you.)
* Are you allowing your journal writing to develop your instincts – your 'sense' of what's good for your life? Are you letting yourself *trust* your instincts? This may mean you are asking others less often for their opinions.

* What talents or interests is your journal writing supporting?
* Are there relationships or connections in your life that need more enthusiasm? Are there events that need your understanding and forgiveness? Have you been writing about that? Describe any inner obstacles or conflicts, or insights and achievements?
* Are there any relationships or connections in your life that need more distance? Have you been writing about that?
* Are you anchoring your insights by writing them down?
* Are you looking for the emotions that drive complex situations?
* Are you celebrating joys? And writing about them?
* Where could you still do with some internal loosening up? Are you ready to write about that?
* You inevitably influence and affect other people. Does that feature yet in these pages? Again, try writing something from the point of view of someone you find 'difficult' to understand. Or write them a letter in the pages of this journal — not to send, but to broaden your own perspective.
* How happy are you with the amount of time that you are giving to your journal writing? Is this a generous investment? Are you getting back an adequate return?
* Think back to your original intention in writing this journal. At least every three months or so, review that original intention and bring it up to date by writing about it. That alone will tell a fascinating story.
* If your journal writing has been half-hearted, write about that. What does it tell you? Be curious rather than self-critical.
* Explore the differences between 'noticing', 'reviewing' and 'judging'.

Your turn

Use just one of the jumping-off points on the previous pages to deepen your knowledge of your own unique inner world — and how you respond to the outer world.

Choose instinctively.

Give yourself time to reflect on whichever question reaches out to you.

Incorporate those reflections in your journal writing.

Remember that it's much easier to discern patterns than individual responses. Let yourself look with interest for small clues. Let yourself grow subtle in your reflections.

Note where and when you are writing. ('Just got the kids to bed. Jack wanted more and more stories . . .')

Note your hopes for this topic. ('I'm looking for simple joys — not at the big questions I am usually focusing on . . .')

Be aware of what's going on in your body. Write about that.

If you notice strong emotions or associations arising as you write, include them in your writing.

Write instinctively and freely.

Write for at least 20 minutes.

Don't edit or rewrite.

At the end of your journal entry, complete this sentence: 'I didn't expect to discover . . .'

Don't re-read immediately.

Let your thoughts 'rest'.

* This is a section in your journal you
  will return to many times. Choose or
  make a striking bookmark to use to
  mark your place here.

* Whenever you feel unfocused, come
  back to this section. Let it inspire
  you. When it doesn't, write about
  what that's like.

'The taste was that of the crumb of madeleine which . . . my aunt Leonie used to give me, dipping it first in her own cup of real or of limeflower tea.'

Marcel Proust

* Review your original motivation in
  writing this journal.

* Does your approach to journal writing
  echo the way you do other things?

* What would free your creativity
  even more?

120

120

* Try dialoguing with 'nothing'.
  What are you? Where have you come from? What do you want to tell me?
  Write down both sides of the conversation. Listen carefully to 'nothing'!

'I have one outstanding trait in my character . . . I can watch myself and my
actions, just like an outsider.'

Anne Frank

_____

_____

_____

_____

_____

_____

_____

_____

_____

_____

_____

_____

_____

_____

_____

* Keep a note of whatever patterns you
   are observing. ('Lots about work.')
   Don't judge. Just comment.

* Are you able to 'review' without
   falling into old patterns of self-
   criticism? Don't criticise yourself
   for that! Just notice – and write
   about it.

Writing about 'nothing'

'Nothing' has a big part to play in journal writing. 'Nothing' is often where 'something' is hiding. Similarly, 'nowhere' frequently leads you to the perfect 'somewhere'.

Christopher Robin and Winnie the Pooh describe this in A. A. Milne's *The House at Pooh Corner*:

'Where are we going?' said Pooh, hurrying after [Christopher Robin] . . .

'Nowhere,' said Christopher Robin.

So they began going there, and after they had walked a little way Christopher Robin said, 'What do you like doing best in the world, Pooh?'

'Well,' said Pooh, 'what I like best' — and then he had to stop and think about eating honey, visiting Christopher Robin, being with Piglet, humming along . . .

'I like that too,' said Christopher Robin, 'but what I like doing best is Nothing.'

'How do you do Nothing?' asked Pooh, after he had wondered for a long time.

'Well, it's when people call out at you as you're going off to do it, "What are you going to do, Christopher Robin?" and you say, "Oh, nothing," and then you go and do it.'

'Oh, I see,' said Pooh.

'This is a nothing sort of thing that we're doing now.'

'Oh, I see,' said Pooh again.

'It means just going along, listening to all the things you can't hear, and not bothering.'

'Oh!' said Pooh.

Exploring 'nothing'

All too often people say, 'I'd like to write a journal, but I'm afraid that I would have nothing to say.' As Manesh shows, this is seldom true.

> ### MANESH
>
> 'I did keep a diary for years but it was just a shorthand account of events. I read other people's journals like Anais Nin, Katherine Mansfield, Anne Frank. And of course, Boswell and Proust. I found their diaries far more interesting than reading novels or biographies and, maybe it was because their insights were so *exquisite*, it intimidated me. My life felt frankly dull next to theirs. But the funny thing was that it was only when I got going and started to write what I call my "real" journal that I could also see that many of the things that those greats paid attention to were also trivial and unremarkable in and of themselves. They became beautiful or meaningful because they were being *noticed*.
>
> 'What made a difference for me, funnily enough, was studying still-life painting as a hobby. The objects we painted were everyday objects as is often true with still-life. One day, though, I could see the connection that seems so obvious now between journal writing and still-life painting. Both art forms – and I regard them as art – invite you to pause. What I am recording when I write in my journal are a whole series of *pauses* and really and truly nothing else is needed.'

One of the most effective ways to write a lot about 'something' is to try to force yourself to write about 'nothing'! (Try now, for a moment, to think about 'nothing' and discover how impossible it is.) This is partly because 'nothing' always has a particular subjective meaning. It is also because we humans are incurably and wonderfully contrary.

Even when we are aware that an instruction is 'paradoxical' ('Do NOT think of a yellow canary . . .'), our minds grab onto paradoxical suggestions and begin to play without further prompting.

Often 'nothing' is a kind of veil: we need to draw it aside and look behind it to find out where 'something' is hiding. Sometimes 'nothing' is also a defence: against feeling or even against thinking. It can even be a kind of passive aggression that shuts other people out or punishes them:

'What's wrong?'

'Nothing.'

'Can I help?'

'No.'

'Is there anything that I can do for you?'

'Probably not.'

When 'nothing' occupies your mind, or you feel stuck in a mire of negativity, take at least as much interest in what's going on as when you are filled with ideas and eager to write. This will give you a dramatic demonstration of how 'thoughts' are really energy forms.

As you write, the energy of 'nothing' will always change into something else. You will feel it — not simply perceive it.

Your turn

Choose any one of these prompts.

* '"Nothing" right now feels like . . .'
* 'Buried inside "nothing" are these emotions . . .'
* '"Nothing" is a big blanket that lets me hide from . . .'
* 'I hate it when I ask people what's wrong and they say, "Nothing".'
* 'I'm the kind of person who will say that nothing's wrong when it is not true.'
* 'I like to be clear about everything at least a day / month / year in advance.'
* 'You're a big NOTHING . . .'
* 'The best time I ever had doing nothing was when . . .'
* 'I often feel I have nothing to contribute when . . .'
* 'If nothing could smell, it would smell like . . .'
* 'If nothing had a taste, it would be . . .'
* 'If I were to hold "nothing" in my hands, it would feel like . . .'
* '"Nothing" and "nowhere" are lonely experiences for me.'
* 'The devil makes work for idle hands.'
* 'I envy people who have time to do nothing . . .'
* 'I have too much "nothing" in my life.'
* 'I don't know whether "nothing" is an outside experience or an inside one.
* 'What it's like for me is . . .'

Note where and when you are writing. ('First thing in the morning. Still dark. At the dining table.')
Note any familiar associations with 'nothing'. Write them down.
Note your mood or sense of anticipation. What would you like to discover?
Give yourself time to reflect on the prompt you have chosen. Just drift with it.
Be aware of what's going on in your body. ('Have barely got going yet . . .')
Let yourself write instinctively and freely.

If you notice strong emotions or associations arising as you write, include them in your writing. ('Dad was the one who was always on our backs to do something, however boring it was. I hated that, but I drive myself by keeping busy also. Even writing in this diary when surely there is something that is far more important to be doing still causes me to feel anxious sometimes as though nothing I do just for myself is really something of value . . .')
Write for at least 20 minutes.
Don't edit or rewrite.
Finish by completing this sentence: 'Nothing led me to . . .'
Don't re-read immediately.
Let your thoughts 'rest'.

Return to the same topic tenaciously until you are confident that you really have got 'something' out of 'nothing'.

'It's hard to think back in a journal, so much happens each day. That week in the Midwest already seems far off. But what remains vivid now is the memory of the plains . . . and on the last day a visit to Ethel Seybold's ancient farm . . . She and her sister work at it as if it were a poem.'

May Sarton

✳ 'Nothing' always has a shape.
Watch that shape inside your mind
with your eyes closed. Then watch
how that shape changes and
becomes something else.
Then write about it.

'A woman stood on her back step,
arms folded, waiting.'

Doris Lessing

* 'Nothing' is a first reaction, perhaps
a defence. Regard it with curiosity.
Go into it. Don't be put off.

* What is the 'something' you hope to
  find inside your 'nothing'?

* What's standing between you and
  'something'?

* Does thinking about 'something'
  make you feel more like 'someone'?

'It's dark already and I'm out here again, talking,
telling the story to the quiet night.'

Tim Winton

Unfinished business

We all have it: unfinished business. One of the greatest gifts journal writing can offer is the chance not necessarily to 'finish' that business, but to understand it better. (And ourselves.)

Isabelle talks about her 'unfinished business' like this.

ISABELLE

'I was raised by my grandmother and she died when I was 17. I had some counselling in my twenties and thirties but I can honestly say that one of the best things I ever did was writing a series of letters to Nan over a period of about eight months. I did it after I lost a close friend of my own age and felt terribly confronted by death all over again. I had really blamed myself that I was horrible to Nan in the year before she died and that I didn't do enough for my friend Danny either. That guilt is still with me but not in anything like the same way. I probably wrote about nine or ten letters in all. I've never re-read them, but I honestly felt like Nan knew exactly what I was saying to her. I spoke to her through my heart and it was astonishingly releasing. I've got the letters in a journal and it's almost like having a communication there *from* her, even though I wrote them.'

Write out whatever thoughts occur to you in response to the suggestions below. Don't converse in your mind only. Put it all on paper.

Some practical suggestions

* Move slowly. There are probably deep emotions swirling around, some of them unconscious. Treat yourself compassionately.
* Perhaps start out by doing nothing more than making notes on the pages that follow about what your unfinished business is.
* Later on you may choose to record what attempts you have already made to get more insight. And what benefits that reaped.
* Record what your hopes are. ('It would help me most to be able to think about this less intensely.' 'I'd like to feel confident that I could look Jess in the eye and say . . .')
* Look at the obstacles that lie between you and that outcome. Are they self-made?
* Could you 'bless the obstacle' – at least for the breathing space it has given you?
* Are you ready to dissolve the obstacle, transform it, or circumvent it?
* You may see things differently on different days. Just notice that with interest.
* Leave plenty of time to let any new insight mature. No rushing.
* Ask yourself what 'finishing this business' would feel like. Sometimes our old pains and grudges are familiar and have their uses. But generally speaking they also have a use-by date. It's liberating to know when that is.
* Explore what lies beyond 'finished'.

'Finishing' – like journal writing itself – has its own integrity and inner timetable. Your conscious mind can want something to be decisively over and finished with, yet your unconscious mind may still be gnawing away at it.

Writing about a complex situation is a highly effective way to bring those conscious and unconscious processes closer together, especially when you can do so without feeling that things must be resolved in a particular way or within a particular time frame.

Joe found writing an unposted letter (as part of his journal writing) illuminating and helpful.

JOE

'Two years after my marriage ended, I wrote a long letter to my ex-wife in my journal to try to heal some of my pain. I wrote it and then put it away for about a month. I couldn't even bear to get the journal out during that time. When I did get it out again I wrote another draft. This went on for several more weeks. What I discovered was that I had to forgive myself more than my wife. We are both good people who got caught up in a spiral that said a lot about our inexperience. She left me for someone else and that was devastating. But my capacity to be a loving partner had also got lost along the way [in the marriage]. In that way, I'd also left her. Writing about it also brought back the good times that I had kind of forgotten. It was extremely hard to do – but yes, certainly worth it. And no, I didn't ever post the letter. It didn't seem right to do so. I'm moving on.'

'Journal writing is crucial to recognising those parts of ourselves that we have shunned. Unconsciousness needs the eye of consciousness.'

Marion Woodman

Your turn

Note the details as you begin writing. ('Back in the red chair.')

Note your state of mind — right now. ('I don't know where to begin . . .')

Take time to reflect on the nature of your 'unfinished business'.

You may want to deal just with the easiest aspect of it. That's fine.

Be sure to note the hopes that arise with your choice.

Explore the suggestions on page 135.

Choose any one of them instinctively and focus on it for your entire journal writing session.

Note the emotions you feel right now.

You don't need to write anything 'important'.

You don't even need to write complete sentences.

You may want to start by just 'free associating': allowing a string of words to jump from your mind onto the page.

Be aware of what's going on in your body. ('I don't want to remember but this follows me around anyway and gives me headaches . . .')

Write for at least 20 minutes.

Don't edit or rewrite.

You may also want to:

1. *Write a letter or a series of letters, either to the person involved or to the situation itself. Do NOT post these letters. They belong in your journal.*

2. *Write a letter to yourself from the point of view of anyone else involved. This may bring you unexpected insights.*

3. *Write a letter of advice to yourself from the perspective of someone whose wisdom you esteem.*

Don't re-read what you have written immediately.

Let your thoughts 'rest'.

Take your time with this.

You may want to write about other topics in the meantime.

'Vision is infinitely greater than baggage.'

Stephen R. Covey

IDYLLES ET ÉLÉGIES

Sans prévenir, elle dit ... me voilà
Ce cœur m'attend. Par l'Amour que
Comme autrefois j'y viens régner en
Au nom d'amour ma raison se troubl
Je voulus fuir, et tout mon corps tre
Je bégayai des plaintes au perfide.
Pour me toucher il prit un air timide
Puis à mes pieds, en pleurant, il tom

✳ Is 'finishing' generally an issue for you?

✳ The idea of 'closure' is highly subjective. Sometimes moving on is the best we can do.

✳ Resentment is a 'normal' emotion
  that is profoundly destructive.
  It can be left behind.

✳ Are there forgiveness issues here?

✳ Any fool can blow up a bridge.
  It takes courage to mend them.

'Difficulties present choices. we can either waste away from our wounds
or use them to grow our souls.'

Joan Borysenko

'There are hundreds of ways to kneel and kiss the earth.'

Jalal-ud-din Rumi

* Move slowly. Let patterns emerge.

'Thou hast battled for the right / With many a brave and trenchant word / And shown us how the pen may fight / A mightier battle than the sword.'

Phoebe Cary

✳ Write a letter to a person or a
situation in this journal – for your
own sake, no-one else's.

Letting problems 'rest'

Your journal can be a place to 'rest' a problem, leaving it to your unconscious mind to sort out and giving your conscious mind a welcome break.

It can also create invaluable boundaries so that you think about your problem only while you are writing about it – and not otherwise. (It can't ruin your entire day.)

It helps to write out in detail what the issue is. ('I can't decide whether to give up this job, which is boring but safe, or just risk the new job even though it's for three months only.')

It may even be appropriate at this point to write out what the positives are for each or every possible decision.

You may want to do this as a list. You can also do it as a letter to your journal, convincing your journal of one viewpoint, and then the other. ('Dear Journal, I know that job security is more important to me than anything else and as I am 35 and have a mortgage no-one could argue with that . . .')

Writing out the problem can already be illuminating. Don't pick at it. Trust your intuition. Trust your unconscious mind. Problems have their own timetable. Some problems are better solved by time than a conscious decision.

Your turn

Note the details as you start to write. ('3 a.m. Can't sleep so may as well write.')

Note your state of mind — right now.

Take time to state what the problem is. (Even if you have already written about it, start afresh. You are encouraging the clarity of your 'beginner's mind'.)

You may want to deal just with the easiest aspect of it.

Be sure to note precisely what you hope for. ('Just want to be able to set it aside.')

Note the familiar emotions associated with this problem or this kind of problem. ('Feel worse because . . .')

You may want to start by 'free associating': allowing a string of words to jump from your mind onto the page.

Be aware of what's going on in your body.

Write for at least 20 minutes.

Don't stop to edit or rewrite.

You may also want to:

1. *Write out a detailed dialogue between your Rational Self and your Intuitive Self. (R: 'You ought to . . .' I: 'My hunch is . . .')*
2. *Look at the problem from the perspective of a year from now; then five years from now. Write in as much detail as you can.*
3. *Write about the problem from the point of view of someone you regard as exceptionally wise.*
4. *Write a letter to your journal about the problem.*
5. *Write about the problem in the third person. ('Francine thinks she wants to retire early . . .')*

Accept that you may not be ready yet to 'solve your problem'.

Write about what it would feel like if this problem is never solved.

Try writing: 'I would prefer to have this problem solved but it is not essential.'

Does that feel possible? Explore how that feels.

Don't re-read what you have written immediately.

Let your thoughts 'rest'.

Take your time with this.

You may want to write about other topics in the meantime.

'Some Sunday mornings you'll find me at the Greek Orthodox church, even though I am neither Greek nor Orthodox . . . I am consciously putting myself into a place where richness comes to me in a way that's beyond words.'

Robert Fulghum

* Name your problem for clarity's sake.

* Review your original motivation in
solving this problem.

'I've found that keeping a daily journal or writing a daily poem is a wonderful way to stay in touch with what's important to me and who I want to be.'

Bernie Siegel

﹡ Look at the hurdles to solving this
problem. Describe them. (Circumvent
them?) How familiar is this impasse?
How have you got through this kind
of situation before?

* Note small shifts in your point of view.

* Set limits to your 'problem-solving
  time'. Keep to those limits.

'Twenty-four brand new hours are before me.'

Thich Nhat Hanh

✳ Choose beautiful paper for your
  additional writing. Keep it here, in or
  with your journal

⃰ Respect your progress.

'We create heaven or hell through our own responses.'

Polly Young-Eisendrath

* Feel free to move between sections of
this journal, developing new ideas.
Use your instincts as a guide

* Date your entries. And always note
your state of mind

The opposite may also be true

'The two hardest things to handle in life are failure and success.'

Anon

Many years ago, when I was first training in psychotherapy, we were asked to do an apparently simple little exercise that basically consisted of looking at a few cards drawn from a tarot pack and then describing a single card in great detail from a negative and then from a positive point of view.

Of course the point of the exercise was to challenge the way that all of us fall into the rut of our own lazy assumptions. Most of us routinely think in divisive ways (good/bad, black/white). We find it hard to remember that most situations are complex and contain all kinds of elements: favourable and less favourable – depending on your perspective.

Many painful, difficult or 'tricky' situations can be eased wonderfully if you approach them less defensively and with curiosity.

Seeing 'all sides of the story' won't make you a wishy-washy person, but it may make you a wiser one. You may even have the same point of view as when you started, but you will be less aggressive about it and more flexible. And where you can concede a point, or understand where someone else is coming from, in most situations you will find that their attitude will also soften.

Your turn

Note where and when you are writing. ('On the ferry. Cold and wet.')
Note your state of mind — right now. ('This feels like very thin ice . . .')
Take a few moments to reflect on any complex situation where you feel somewhat 'stuck'.
Identify what you need or want: solution, inspiration, fresh perspective, flexibility, courage.
Be sure to note emotions and thoughts, and also the hopes that arise as you begin to reflect.
You don't need to write anything 'important'.
You don't even need to write whole sentences.
You may want to start by 'free associating': allowing a string of words to jump from your mind onto the page.

Follow these steps.
(You will probably cover one step only in a single journal writing session.)
1. Describe the situation from your point of view. Give yourself time to reflect on the issue. Get down every point that will support your view. Explore the emotions that are driving your arguments. Do you understand why this matters so much to you? Write about that also.
2. Now write about your desired outcome. What will it achieve? What will it do for you? Write about it as though it has happened. ('I am so thrilled

that I finally managed to convince Ted to go on holiday . . .')

3. Now write about the outcome as though you did not get what you are hoping for. What will that be like for you? Write about it as though it has already happened. ('I never did manage to convince Ted to go on holiday and it seems like this is the last time that I want to concede something so important to me . . .')

4. Now write about the situation from the point of view of whoever else is involved. Take your time with this. Sit like that person. Use their language. Try to get thoroughly 'in character', physically as well as mentally. Too bad if this seems silly! It can be extraordinarily helpful. ('I hate seeing Marg so angry, but I feel like neither one of us has room to say what we really want without offending the other one . . .')

You may also want to write a 'letter' in this journal either to someone else involved or to the situation itself. ('Dear Ideal Holiday . . .')

Don't mail it or even talk about it — especially not until you are quite sure that you are not attacking or self-justifying.

If you have a lot of energy around difficult emotions, fantasise about what the 'opposite' emotion might be. And what it would give you. Write about that.

Let yourself write instinctively and freely.

If you notice strong emotions or associations arising as you write, include them in your writing.

Don't re-read immediately.

Don't edit or rewrite.

Let your thoughts 'rest'.

* Strong minds are also flexible.
  Let preconceptions go.

* Situations that really churn us up
  usually have a long history.
  Respect that – but don't feel
  inhibited by it.

***

Sans prevenir, elle dit... me voilà
Ce cœur m'attend. Par l'Amour que
Comme autrefois j'y viens régner en
Au nom d'amour ma raison se trouble
Je voulus fuir, et tout mon corps tre
Je bégayai des plaintes au perfide.
Pour me toucher il prit un air timide
Puis à mes pieds, en pleurant, il tom

'The daily journal is like a mirror. When we first look into it, the blank pages stare back with ominous emptiness. But if we keep looking . . . gradually we begin to see the face that is looking back at us.'

Marion Woodman

✳ Explore your general attitudes about
'being right' or 'being wrong'. Let
yourself be surprised.

* Sometimes we 'land' the emotions
  from one situation onto another
  inappropriately. It's good to do
  some weeding.

* Conceding a point (or two) often
  hastens the way forward.

'It's all right not to be clear.'

Robert Aitken

* If something really 'gets you going',
  it is worth writing about.

* As we get older we have the *choice*
  to become wiser. It doesn't happen
  automatically!

'If you could understand the wonderful mixture of strength and weakness with which the things I love fill me! It's what I call the caress of happiness.'

Colette

Recording quotations and comments

Many journal writers are also keen readers. It adds invaluable texture to your journal writing to use your journal as a place to keep notes about books that you have read, plays and movies that you have seen, music you are listening to. I strongly urge you to do this on sheets of paper that you can then keep between the pages of this journal. *Be sure to date them.* It's invaluable also to make a brief comment about what interested you. ('Was looking for something about preventing colds – then sat for hours reading about folk cures instead of writing my speech for tomorrow's sales conference.')

Simply recording what you have heard, seen or read can never give you the same vivid picture that a brief commentary will. It's that brief commentary that is reflecting your own intimate personal life back to you.

Your journal is also an ideal place to write out passages from books or articles that are especially meaningful for you. I have been writing out notes from other people's books for years and know that these notes also come to tell an invaluable 'story'. I have used them directly in my writing and as an unparalleled source of inspiration from the 'unceasing conversation' that takes place between readers and writers, across countries, cultures and centuries. There have been chunks of time when I didn't do this – and I genuinely regret those gaps. (And am reminded of one of my favourite quotes, now committed to memory, from one of my all-time favourite writers, Joseph Campbell: '*Regrets are illuminations come too late.*')

Writing out a poem, for example, gives you a quite different experience from simply reading it. Writing it out, then reading it aloud, takes you much closer to the poet's own processes of discovery. It also often makes it clear to you why this particular piece of writing had meaning for your life. *Note that.*

> ### ROLAND
> 'I read a lot of inspirational autobiographies, but for a long time I was reading them as though those people's existence had nothing to do with me. I admired them from afar, looked up to them, if you will. I started jotting quotes down when I joined a Toastmasters Group to practise public speaking and then started writing the journal at about the same time. So I also began to question, "Why this quote? What did this person really mean to me? What was I unconsciously seeking to understand?" It gave me an emotional depth to my reading that I know I didn't have before and it also made me realise how important courage is to me: that it's the value I care most about. I kind of like that about myself. It brought it home.'

In his published journal, *The Road to Daybreak*, Henri J. M. Nouwen makes many references to his reading. They add tremendous depth to the 'inner' conversation he is having with himself as the journal writer (and eventually with us, his readers).

'Just a week after I had bought some postcards with reproductions of paintings by Cézanne, Rainer Maria Rilke's *Letters on Cézanne* was sent to

me as a Christmas gift. It is a happy coincidence.
I have felt a deep connection with Rilke. Now he
will introduce me to Cézanne . . . Rilke will
help me to see.'

The Scottish poet, William Soutar, also offers a vivid example of how
worthwhile it is to include thoughts about reading in your writing.
By an odd coincidence he, too, is reflecting on reading the personal
writing of a nineteenth-century French painter.

'Finished reading *The Intimate Journals of Paul
Gauguin*. Very fresh mind — he at once joins the
company of those whom we wish we could have
met. Such a distinctive French book makes a Scot
[Soutar] feel that he is a rather dog-collared dog.'

Your turn

* *Write your quotations directly into your journal or on separate pieces of
  paper to be pressed between the pages of your journal.*
* *Date them — and also note where you were when you read the book or
  article and maybe what else you were doing at that time. You will forget
  those details surprisingly quickly and all kinds of memories will come
  rushing back when you look back and remember that you read a
  particularly moving poem while on holiday with friends you have known
  since your school days.*
* *Occasionally reflect and write about what emotions or associations the
  quotation calls up for you. ('I'd like to live in that highly principled way,
  but the reality is I am barely managing to be pleasant to my family right
  now . . .')*

* You may also want to 'respond' by writing a poem or prose piece yourself. Or making a drawing. Or finding a piece of music that 'fits' what you have read.
* If you find something exceptionally inspiring, send it on to friends by email. Or write it onto a card and send it to one person only — perhaps someone you are struggling to appreciate.
* Treasure your collection of quotations. Regard your treasure-hunting as an activity that will add texture to all of your journal writing — as something to take up regularly.

'I have been in Paradise all month, reading Virginia Woolf's fourth volume of letters and the biography of E. M. Forster, grazing with immense pleasure in those rich pastures. We all have our ideas of Heaven.'

May Sarton, *Recovering: A Journal*

＊ Be guided by your instincts: 'This
interests me.'

'It is fatal not to write the thing one wants to write at the moment of wanting to write it.'

Virginia Woolf

'I'm awfully scared that everyone who knows me as I always am will discover that I have another side, a finer and better side. I'm afraid they'll laugh at me, think I'm ridiculous and sentimental, not take me seriously.'

Anne Frank

* Collecting quotations may inspire
  you to read more widely.

* The most powerful ideas are often
  best expressed in poetry.

* Allow yourself to be moved by what
  is beautiful.

'To love unconditionally is to respond radically to life.'

Matthew Fox

'I think these difficult times have helped me to understand better than before how infinitely rich and beautiful life is in every way and that so many things that one goes around worrying about are of no importance whatsoever.'

Isak Dinesen

* Keep adding 'texture', colour, depth.
Let your journal reflect your life.

'Our deepest fear is not that we are inadequate. Our deepest fear
is that we are powerful beyond measure.'

Marianne Williamson

IDYLLES ET ÉLÉGIES

Sans prévenir, elle dit : « Me voilà.
Ce cœur m'attend. Par l'Amour que
Comme autrefois j'y viens régner enc
Au nom d'amour ma raison se troubl
Je voulus fuir, et tout mon corps tre
Je bégayai des plaintes au perfide.
Pour me toucher il prit un air timide
Puis à mes pieds, en pleurant, il tom

✳ Note where you found your quotation, and when, as well as why it interests you.

Making lists and resolutions

On tiny scraps of paper I still have my New Year resolutions carefully recorded from several years before I had my children and my whole life changed. ('Write more, worry less' and 'Work less, exercise more' seem to be consistent themes.)

Any kind of list like that – one that registers your hopes and goes some way towards ordering your priorities – adds precious texture to your journal writing and is legitimately part of your journey of self-discovery.

If you feel particularly driven by other people's expectations, or your own superego (that voice inside saying you *should*, you *ought*, you *must*), it can be truly liberating literally to record those injunctions and instructions as lists. Until you get them out of your head and heart and down in black and white on the page, it can be difficult to challenge or make sense of them. And move on.

Towards the end of her book, *Navigating Midlife*, Robyn Vickers-Willis writes:

'This morning I picked up my journal and read an entry in it for the first time since writing it this time last year. I was surprised to read: "And now at the end of this millennium my big goal is to write about where I have come from and where I want to go." I had no idea I was thinking that way a year ago. Oh! The value of keeping a journal. . . I can now see that for months, if not years before I started writing, there was a force within me suggesting that this was something I needed to do.'

On 1 January 1915, seven years before her death at the age of thirty-four, Katherine Mansfield wrote:

'What a vile little diary! But I am determined to keep it this year. We saw the Old Year out and the New Year in. A lovely night, blue and gold . . . For this year I have two wishes: to write, to make money. Consider. With money we could go away as we liked, have a room in London, be as free as we liked, and be independent and proud with nobodies. It is only poverty that holds us so tightly. Well, J. [John Middleton Murry, her husband] doesn't want money and won't earn money. I must. How? First, get this book finished [a novel she in fact eventually abandoned]. That is a start. When? At the end of January. If you do that, you are saved. If I wrote night and day I could do it. Yes I could. Right O!

'I feel the new life coming nearer. I believe, just as I always have believed. Yes, it will come. All will be well.'

Your turn

* *Don't save your resolutions only for New Year. Make them regularly. Review them compassionately.*
* *Look for patterns. Do they reflect your best interests?*
* *Exercise choice. This supports the fact that your life is largely what you make of it.*
* *Are your resolutions inspiring or intimidating?*
* *Record your 'shoulds' and 'oughts' in relation to a particular situation. ('I should be better dressed.' 'I ought to get a promotion.') When you have them down in black and white it becomes much easier to see whether they serve you well, or not.*
* *Be clear who you are aiming to please — or impress.*
* *Is there room in your life for joy, creativity and care for nature, as well as time to show your care for other people?*
* *Make some resolutions from the point of view of your body or your soul or your spirit. They might surprise you.*
* *Know what your strengths are. Note and write about them. Develop them.*

* Do your resolutions inspire you?
If not, back to the drawing board.

'I have a dream that my four little children will one day live in a nation where they will not be judged by the colour of their skin but by the content of their character.'

Martin Luther King

* Think about your values. How does
  your life reflect them?

* Better to fail nobly than to succeed
  at an unworthy task.

'Part of living with love is also learning how to say "no".'

Bernie Siegel

✳ Imagine the resolutions of the
people you admire most.
Write them down.

'It takes courage to do what you want. Other people have a lot of plans for you.'

Joseph Campbell

194

* Are you keeping some everyday lists
  and notes? They also tell a story.

* Honour the details.

'One of the most important relationships in your life is with your soul. Will you be kind and loving to your soul, or will you be harsh and difficult?'

Elisabeth Kübler-Ross

TIME TO BE

'Yesterday was a strange, hurried, uncentred day; yet I did not
have to go out, the sun shone. Today I feel centered and time is
a friend instead of the old enemy. It was zero this morning. I have
a fire burning in my study, yellow roses and mimosa on my desk.
There is an atmosphere of festival, of release, in the house. We are
one, the house and I, and I am happy to be alone — time to think,
time to be.'

May Sarton, Journal of a Solitude

Putting it all together

Savour your entire life

Your conscious memory is a treasure house. Filled with even greater treasures is your unconscious mind. There all kinds of infinitely precious experiences and impressions from the first moments of your life are faithfully stored. Some of these unconscious treasures are revealed to you through your dreams, if you remember them. They are also revealed through moments of synchronicity or coincidence, when a book like this one 'falls off the shelf'; your 'slips of the tongue', when you say something your conscious mind 'didn't mean to'; your 'free associations', many of which are developed in this journal.

———————————

Your creativity, too, draws very directly on your unconscious mind, which is often way ahead of your conscious mind in its breadth, depth, honesty and precision.

Journal writing not only develops your creativity (as well as your intuition, decision-making, self-awareness and self-confidence), it is itself a highly creative activity that offers you one of the most direct means available to uncover and yield up the 'secrets' of your unconscious mind. It lets you bring more of your experience into conscious awareness. It lets you retrieve what you have forgotten or previously set aside. IT LETS YOU SEE WHAT YOU HAD 'NOT NOTICED'.

Broadening your vision and perspective in this way, you will experience the whole of your life more richly and fully. Writing freely – free of self-censorship and self-criticism – you will always go beyond what you already know. You will always surprise yourself. You will always make fresh connections. You may even experience unexpected healing. And your life will feel more 'of a piece'.

It is easy to understand why so many people are afraid to explore their unconscious mind. They mistakenly believe that what is buried there is only their pain, or their darker thoughts and experiences. Sometimes too they worry that if they begin to feel a little of that pain, their conscious defences will come crashing down and they will feel intolerably exposed. Or even that they might hate themselves if they were to remember what they have tried to forget.

But journal writing shows you very clearly that any discoveries you make will evolve at a pace that is easy for you to deal with. What's more, as you do so, this will support a feeling of being more integrated, more in touch with all of who you are.

'Not remembering' or 'disowning' parts of your life takes energy. Some of what you remember or find yourself writing about may eventually be quite sad. It may also be your finest hopes, your deepest desires, GLIMPSES OF YOUR OWN GREATNESS! Or it may be hilarious. Or shocking.

Whatever evolves, 'remembering' and reintegrating the past releases energy in the present.

This is how Judith describes it.

JUDITH

'I am the most practical of people. I wouldn't even have said that I was especially interested in knowing what's going on at the deeper levels. But I have been astonished to find how rich some of my memories are once I began writing about them. All kinds of things that I hadn't thought about for years just tumbled out onto the page. I know that if I was just telling a story or an anecdote about my life I'd never get into that kind of detail. I'd be too self-conscious for one thing. But no-one gets to read my journal and I can let myself get right into it.

'I suppose I did think that most of what was buried away was the sad stuff, but I tell you, sometimes I am sitting there chuckling away like a mad woman, and it's like I have that moment right here, in the palm of my hand.'

'I am getting fine and supple from the mistakes I have made but I wish a notebook could laugh.'

Florida Scott-Maxwell

Back to the big picture

When the English fiction writer Jean Rhys found herself unable to work, she turned to her diary:

> 'This time I must not blot a line. No revision, no
> second thoughts. Down it shall go. Already I am
> terrified. No row of pencils, no pencil sharpener,
> no drink. The standing jump.'

Journal writing will make you more engaged with your own life. (And it will develop your curiosity about how you are affecting and influencing other people.) Keeping a journal, you won't fear that your own life is passing you by. You can capture your experiences, think about them, understand them.

Your journal writing empowers you in other ways too. It lets you live your life at depth, rather than skating on the surface from one experience to the next with no time to reflect, savour, learn. In that sense, journal writing is a deeply unfashionable activity. It defies superficiality — even when a lot of what you write may be relatively superficial at first glance.

It pushes you also to think with your heart and feel with your mind. It lets you experience how mind and heart are linked. Learning to 'read' your life as an outsider as well as an insider, learning to reflect on and interpret the details of your life, may be the first big change that journal writing will give you.

But that's not all. There will also be the gifts of emotional release, of creativity, of problem-solving.

And it's important to remember that looking for and finding the 'big picture' is also part of journal writing. This can be particularly useful if you tend to get lost in detail or repetition. Journal writing will soon make that clear to you. It will help you to discern what is important and what is not; what feels 'stuck'; and how to write your way out of problems.

Combine many strands

Most journal writers tend to follow some kind of chronology in their journal and to use their journal to keep track of events as well as impressions of and responses to those events.

I have kept different diaries for different kinds of events sometimes, but now believe the richest periods of journal writing come when the entire mélange of my life lives within the borders of a single journal (and all its inserted pages).

Chronology plus

Your journal is likely to follow some sort of chronology. Neverthe-less, to deepen your understanding of 'events' and to broaden your capacity to initiate and record 'impressions', it is also worth return-ing on a fairly regular basis to some of the exercises in this journal. They will develop your intuition, insight, creativity – and spontaneity. They will help you to 'see' and think differently – and move you out of the rut of linear writing and thinking. Perhaps they will break some of the habits of self-criticism and self-judgement that may initially require your compassion and curious attention.

Adding texture

You can 'write' your journal by drawing, writing stories or poems, following an event in great detail, writing a tiny precis of a complex situation: there is no limit.

In August 1914, Franz Kafka wrote two lines in his diary:

'Germany has declared war on Russia. Swimming
in the afternoon.'

Some of your finest moments of journal writing might occur when you simply string some words together as you 'free associate'. Or you may grow to love the sensual pleasure of choosing whether to note a quotation on paper that is shimmering bold-gold or is fragile duck-egg blue. (Have it all to hand.)

You may find that when you write with your red pen you are franker than when you write in black. You may also find that you write far more when you are away travelling and reflecting on 'home' than when you are physically at home.

Enjoy whatever depth and variety you can bring to your journal writing. Experiment with what delights you most. Your life is a 'work in progress'. So is your journal – and all its living words.

Breaking habits

Journal writing (and reviewing your writing from time to time) will certainly let you see where you have fallen into habits of response or behaviour in your everyday life that are no longer serving you well. ('I can hardly believe I am still blaming Jacob for the way I feel about my body . . .') One of the greatest gifts of journal writing is that it allows you to move on when that would be helpful.

It's worth also checking routinely to make sure that your journal writing itself stays fresh. Make a habit of writing. Make a commitment to write – and keep to it. But vary how you approach whatever you are writing about. (Use the form of a letter; write in the third person; look at it from someone else's point of view; write a story; argue with yourself.)

This is a wonderful opportunity to extend yourself and to experiment in ways that are often discouraged in other areas of your life.

Getting back to it

It helps to know that there is no timetable to follow in journal writing, no 'level' you must get to before journal writing begins to 'work' for you.

Nevertheless, there will be times when you don't write. (Often when you would be getting most from it.) When you 'remember' your journal, don't hesitate to return to it. Take up your journey wherever you left off, approaching it again with curiosity and delight. It marks a renewal of interest in your life and is, paradoxically, also one of the most direct routes out of insularity and self-absorption.

'It depends entirely on yourself how much you see or hear or understand.'

Katherine Mansfield

Your turn

From the moment you pick up a pen and add your own thoughts to this journal, you are a journal writer.

Whatever your topic, take time to reflect on it as though you had never come to it before.

Start by noting why you have chosen 'this', rather than 'that'. ('Writing about singing even though the problems at work are pressing. Too bad.')

If you find you are writing about something else, go with it. There's no agenda in journal writing. It's serving you, no-one else.

Let yourself write instinctively and freely.

If you notice emotions or associations arising as you write, include them in your writing. ('It's really weird that I feel so uplifted right now even though . . .')

Write for at least 20 minutes at any one time. If you are writing fluently and with interest, keep going for as long as you wish.

Don't stop to edit or rewrite.

Be aware of what's going on in your body — and write about that.

At the end of your writing, note any shifts in your state of mind.

Then complete this sentence: 'Insight for the day is . . .' Or: 'I want to know more about . . .'

Don't re-read immediately.

Let your thoughts 'rest'.

There will be days when you want to drift in the company of your journal, rather than write in it. (Or you may want to rearrange your pages; copy out quotations; re-read entries.) On those days, briefly note what you are doing and why it's happening today. Adding texture will make more sense of your choices. ('It's Nell's anniversary and I'm listening to Richard Tognetti playing his violin like a muscular angel . . .')

Key principles

1. Write your journal for yourself — not for anyone else.

2. Write your journal regularly (at least three times a week).

3. Be truthful in your journal.

4. Regard journal writing as a gift to yourself.

5. Respect whatever you discover.

6. Trust yourself — and the contents of your inner world.

Key hints

Sans prévenir, elle dit : « Me voilà !
Ce cœur m'attend. Par l'Amour que
Comme autrefois j'y viens régner enc
Au nom d'amour ma raison se troubl

1. *Choose your topic instinctively. Respond freely.*
2. *Return to the same question or topic for days or weeks on end.*
3. *Know that whatever your 'topic' is, it is allowing you to think more deeply about your own life.*
4. *Don't edit as you write.*
5. *Don't re-read immediately. When you do (once a month or so), look for patterns.*
6. *Write for at least 20 minutes.*
7. *Note if you are constantly writing 'I feel'. Switch to 'I think' or 'I believe'. Or vice versa.*
8. *Regularly write from someone else's perspective (especially someone who mystifies you).*
9. *Regularly ask, 'What am I avoiding?'*
10. *Forget what you wrote yesterday or any other day. Come into* this *day, freshly.*

Difficulties starting or keeping going?

You are writing a journal in part to find out what you don't already know. It helps to remember that bleak and 'boring' patches often precede your greatest insights.

Write your way through them. If you can't write about anything else, then describe how boring they are; what they remind you of; what they are preventing you from discovering.

Or write a letter to them. 'Dear damned Fog, I would like to evict you . . .'

A 'whole-brain' activity

Journal writing usefully – and perhaps uniquely – develops both your so-called 'right-brain strengths' (lateral problem-solving, intuition, creativity, emotions) and your so-called 'left-brain strengths' (intellectual, sequential, rational and orderly thought).

My personal experience is that these functions are so inevitably integrated in journal writing that it becomes a true 'whole-brain' experience. One minute you are writing something about your day that is 'useful' to remember (left brain). Then suddenly you are off, making an association that takes you in an unexpected direction (right brain). From that you may then write down a problem you want to solve (left brain) and that you are prepared to leave to 'cook' until you return to your journal in a day or two (right brain) when, with luck, your unconscious will have solved it for you! But before you finish for the day, you make a quick 'Must do tomorrow' list so that you don't have to think again about those tasks until the morning (left brain, again).

Even more excitingly, sometimes you might find yourself writing about a 'left-brain', rational aspect of your life — work, for example — from a 'right-brain', creative/intuitive angle. Or you may be re-reading your journal to find the patterns, which would seem to be a rather 'left-brain' activity, when actually you are 'following your nose' in a delightfully 'right-brain' kind of way and coming up with 'patterns' way beyond those that initially interested you.

Free from constraints

You may be having difficulties getting started with your journal writing, or keeping it going. Or what you are writing may feel static and predictable.

It is certainly possible to work your way through this. Doing so will benefit your journal writing and give it fresh energy. There will be a secondary gain also. Learning how to write with fewer inhibitions, you will be able to approach all kinds of problem-solving with greater confidence and trust in your own inner resources.

As I know from my own experience, we usually become 'stuck' when our left brain is working overtime (asking us to justify how we could be wasting time journal writing when we could be peeling potatoes, trading futures or working for world peace). At those times, our right brain (creative, intuitive, enjoying the writing process for its own sake) is literally overruled; and the freedom that journal writing needs — and develops — comes to a halt.

So what should you do if this happens?

Dorothea Brande is the author of the famous writing manual,

Becoming a Writer. She doesn't use the left-brain/right-brain terminology referred to here; nevertheless, the strategy she suggests allows you to circumvent your usual left-brain inhibitions very neatly. Right-brain activity (creative, spontaneous, lateral) draws on your less conscious, less censored thoughts and feelings. In fact, says Brande, 'If you are to have the full benefit of the richness of the unconscious, you must learn to write easily and smoothly when the unconscious is in the ascendant.' And the best way to do this?

> 'Rise half an hour, or a full hour, earlier than you customarily rise. Just as soon as you can – and without talking, without reading the morning's paper, without picking up the book you laid aside the night before – begin to write. Write anything that comes into your head: last night's dream, if you are able to remember it; the activities of the day before; a conversation, real or imaginary; an examination of conscience . . . Forget that you have any critical faculty at all . . . Write . . . until you have utterly written yourself out.'

The next day, begin all over again. For your own sake.

'Writer's block results from too much head. Cut off your head. Pegasus, poetry, was born of Medusa when her head was cut off. You have to be reckless when writing. Be as crazy as your conscience allows.'

Joseph Campbell

Further inspiration

The following pages contain 125 possible topics for you to write about.

Whenever you are in need of inspiration, instinctively choose a number between one and 125 and write about that topic, regardless of whether you 'like it' or would consciously have chosen it.

Not 'liking it' is often an excellent way to begin!

Don't forget that you can argue on the page; take opposing or shifting viewpoints; write dialogue or poetry; spend your 'writing time' drawing. It is entirely up to you.

Your turn

Note where and when you are writing. ('Curled up on the sofa in my pyjamas. The city has gone to sleep.')
Note your state of mind — right now. ('Never want to forget today . . .')
Choose your number (between one and 125). That number will give you your topic — accept it!

Take time to reflect on it. Let yourself drift.

Be sure to note the thoughts and the hopes that arose with your choice. ('Odd that I am going to be writing about food when . . .')

Note your old associations with the topic as well as those you feel right now.

Let yourself off the hook. You don't need to write anything important.

You don't even need to write whole sentences.

You may want to start by just 'free associating': allowing a string of words to jump from your mind onto the page.

Be aware of what's going on in your body. ('Can't think about food without feeling hungry. Stomach grumbling right on cue . . .')

Try to write for at least 20 minutes.

Don't edit or rewrite.

End by finishing this sentence: 'I was fascinated to discover . . .'

Let your thoughts rest.

If you can't think what to say, keep writing your key phrase over and over. That may occupy the entire 20 minutes. And it is certainly giving a strong message to your unconscious mind!

Then leave the topic.

You have not wasted your time.

The greatest treasure is often deeply buried.

If you feel 'unfinished', come back to the same topic within a day or so and patiently start all over again. Do so with a 'beginner's mind', as though this topic is entirely new to you.

(Or write about the block itself.)

It is fine to return to the same topic many times.

Your patience will always be rewarded.

Don't forget to choose the number, not the topic.

Increase the element of spontaneity and surprise.

1. *My life as a five-year-old.*
2. *My life as a 95-year-old.*
3. *'What I value most about my life right now is . . .'*
4. *'I am ready to look at . . .'*
5. *'My attitude to money comes from . . .'*
6. *'I have everything I need.'*
7. *'What I want most at this moment is . . .'*
8. *'It's hard for me to say what I want.'*
9. *'What I appreciate most about my gender/sexuality/age is . . .'*
10. *My obituary.*
11. *'What I want most out of life is . . .'*
12. *'People expect me to . . .'*
13. *'I give the impression that . . .'*
14. *'Becoming "myself" would mean . . .'*
15. *'I am sorry about . . .'*
16. *'I am not sorry about . . .'*
17. *'Today, between noon and 1 p.m., this happened.'*
18. *'The best way I know to get over a disappointment is . . .'*
19. *'What life has taught me is that . . .'*
20. *'I feel most in tune with myself when . . .'*
21. *'I'd like to be more generous but . . .'*
22. *'If I were a better person I would . . .'*
23. *'The talent I would develop if I had half a chance is . . .'*
24. *'The qualities that other people admire in me are . . .'*
25. *'If other people could change me, they would want to change . . .'*
26. *'I want to be an encouraging person but . . .'*
27. *'Over the years my values have become . . .'*
28. *'Tuning into my body I'm aware that . . .'*
29. *'I can afford to be wrong about . . .'*
30. *Write (in your journal) a letter to someone no longer in your life.*
31. *Write (in your journal) a letter to someone you hurt.*
32. *Write (in your journal) a letter to someone who hurt you.*

33. *Write (in your journal) a letter to someone who seems very different from you.*
34. *'I am not prejudiced but . . .'*
35. *'I give most of my time to . . .'*
36. *'My life is my own except when . . .'*
37. *'I hurt myself when . . .'*
38. *'I hurt others when. . . .'*
39. *'To me, nurturing the soul means . . .'*
40. *'If I dared to say what I really think . . .'*
41. *'The most crucial aspect of my identity is . . .'*
42. *'The principle I would stand up for is . . .'*
43. *'What I appreciate most is . . .'*
44. *'If someone else looked at my life they would see . . .'*
45. *'The world is dangerous . . .'*
46. *'I can appreciate nature most when . . .'*
47. *'The thing about my own nature is . . .'*
48. *'I can't help . . .'*
49. *'Life is a miracle.'*
50. *'To me a miracle is . . .'*
51. *'My faults have taught me . . .'*
52. *'Loving deeply would mean . . .'*
53. *'I am deeply touched by . . .'*
54. *'I am supported by . . .'*
55. *'My life gets meaning from . . .'*
56. *'What I love most about my friends is . . .'*
57. *'What my friends love most about me is . . .'*
58. *'No-one knows that . . .'*
59. *'Perfection is a reasonable goal . . .'*
60. *'Letting perfection go, I can discover . . .'*
61. *'Pleasing others means . . .'*
62. *'Not pleasing others means . . .'*
63. *'For sheer pleasure I am going to write about . . .'*

64. Unconditional love.

65. The world lives in me.

66. 'My most basic needs are . . .'

67. 'I have learned to live without . . .'

68. 'I could live without . . .'

69. 'I don't want to die without . . .'

70. 'My children/friends/family will remember me for . . .'

71. 'I live by other people's rules . . .'

72. 'I am different from my parents in that . . .'

73. 'I'd like to be different from my parents . . .'

74. 'I am in charge of my own life . . .'

75. 'I am writing this journal because . . .'

76. 'Creativity matters to me more than anything.'

77. 'I didn't get my fair share of creativity. Nevertheless . . .'

78. 'I am making the most of what I have.'

79. 'These are my limits . . .'

80. 'I am most proud of when . . .'

81. 'My creativity is best expressed when . . .'

82. 'I have everything I need.'

83. 'I have the power to . . .'

84. 'Thinking about it again, I . . .'

85. 'I am fine as I am . . .'

86. 'What I love about getting older is . . .'

87. 'Five years ago I didn't know . . .'

88. 'No-one should have to suffer.'

89. 'I shouldn't have to suffer.'

90. 'I want to say "Yes" to . . .'

91. Friendship.

92. 'It is easy for me to be grateful for . . .'

93. Write (in your journal) a letter of thanks.

94. Write (in your journal) a letter of appreciation to someone who annoys you.

95. *Write (in your journal) a letter of appreciation to yourself.*
96. *'The bad habit I am ready to jettison is . . .'*
97. *'Starting from today I can . . .'*
98. *Food.*
99. *Food for the soul.*
100. *Food for the planet.*
101. *Sharing what I have.*
102. *More for me.*
103. *'I need to forgive . . .'*
104. *'I need to ask _____ to forgive me . . .'*
105. *'What I appreciate most about my body is . . .'*
106. *Strangers.*
107. *'I am totally inspired by . . .'*
108. *'I am moved by . . .'*
109. *'Every time I think about joy . . .'*
110. *'Journal writing is giving me . . .'*
111. *'My special gifts are . . .'*
112. *'I have this to give . . .'*
113. *'I have most fun when . . .'*
114. *Self-love.*
115. *'I never thought I would feel so . . .'*
116. *'I want to say "No" to . . .'*
117. *'I will no longer put up with . . .'*
118. *'I have a right to . . .'*
119. *'My responsibilities. . . .'*
120. *'Looking back I can see . . .'*
121. *'Looking forward I can hope . . .'*
122. *Putting things off.*
123. *'I am most myself when . . .'*
124. *'I believe in . . .'*
125. *Write (in your journal) a letter to your closest friend, telling him/her what journal writing has given you.*

Wishing you well

I have enjoyed the adventure of creating this journal enormously.

In fact, it has allowed me to rediscover what I love most about writing, reading and thinking. (What I love includes the creativity of written reflections, as well as the surprises that come from them, the humour, sense of connection, absorption, playfulness, insight, spontaneity, freshness, sense of integrity and self-trust.)

My hope is that you will find it just as exhilarating to pick up where I have left off. That you will find yourself quite inevitably 'dialoguing' with my suggestions and taking off on your own in directions that you cannot yet conceive of or imagine – until you see them on your own pages.

Go well.

You can find out more about my work at
http://www.stephaniedowrick.com

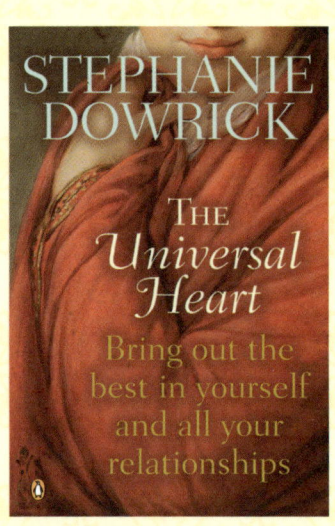

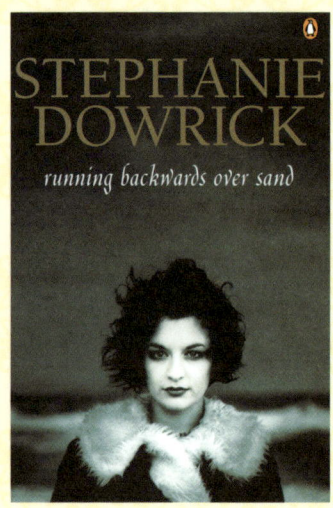

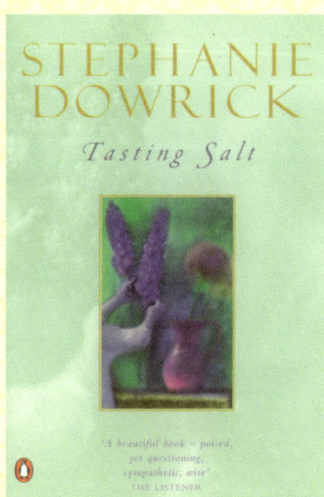